SKOOB *Paci*

Arthur Yap was born in Singapore in 1943. He studied at the University of Singapore, the University of Leeds and obtained his Ph.D. from the National University of Singapore. He has taught in various institutions, including the National University of Singapore.

His first collection of poems, *Only Lines,* was published in 1971, for which he received the National Book Development Council of Singapore's first award for poetry in 1976. He also received the Council's award for *Down the Line* in 1982 and for *Man Snake Apple* in 1988. In 1983, he was awarded the Southeast Asia Write Award in Bankok and the Cultural Medallion for Literature in Singapore.

As an undergraduate and teacher, he has edited and contributed to various journals. Some of his poems have been published as translations in Japanese, Mandarin and Malay.

As a painter, Yap has held 7 solo exhibitions in Singapore as well as participated in group exhibitions in Kuala Lumpur, Bankok and Adelaide.

Arthur Yap

the space of city trees
selected poems

Introduction
by
Anne Brewster
Curtin University

SKOOB BOOKS LTD
LONDON

Copyright © Arthur Yap 2000

Introduction © Anne Brewster 2000

All rights reserved. No part of this publication may be reproduced, stored in a retrieval system, or transmitted in any form by any means without the prior permission of the publisher.

Published in 2000 by
SKOOB BOOKS LTD
15 Sicilian Avenue
Southampton Row
Holborn
London WC1A 2QH

First Edition

ISBN 1 871438 39 X

Printed by WSOY, Finland

British Library Cataloguing-in-Publication data
A Catalogue record for this book is available
from the British Library.

Published with the support of

NATIONAL ARTS COUNCIL
SINGAPORE
Publishing Grant Scheme

for Keith

Acknowledgements

Acknowledgement is made to the following publications in which some of the poems have appeared:

Focus, Singapore
Poetry Singapore, Singapore
Poet, India
New Directions, Singapore
Pacific Quarterly, New Zealand
Ariel, Calgary
Singa, Singapore
Solidarity, Philippines
Southeast Asian Review of English, Malaysia
Tenggara, Malaysia
Westerly, Australia
Look East, Bangkok
Tumasek, Singapore
New Voices of the Commonwealth, London
The Flowering Tree, Singapore
The Second Tongue, Singapore
Literature in English, Ontario
Skoob PACIFICA Anthology, London
Anthology of ASEAN Literatures, Singapore
The Oxford Book of Friendship, London
Journeys: Words, Home and Nation, Singapore

Contents

Introduction   *page* xx

from *Only Lines* (1971)

only lines	3
location	4
sunny day	5
hurrying ahead	6
one road	7
panchor	8
garden episode	9
expansion	10
coming up, flowers	11
perpetual	12
old photographs	13
precedence	14
it rains today	15
old house at ang siang hill	16
in passing	17
readjustment	18
change of pace	19
sunday	20
a scroll painting	21
cameron highlands	22
balancing sounds	23
seasonal	24

from *Five Takes* (1974)

dramatis personae	27
statement	29
fire off kim seng bridge	30
the send-off	31
these sounds, endlessly	32
almost still-life	33
recurrent imagery	34

minimum excavation	35
banyan tree	36
june morning	37
open road	38
evening	39
tanah rata	40

from *Commonplace* (1977)

black & white	45
everything's coming up numbers	46
some friends	47
dog-eared	48
on reading a current best-seller	49
inventory	50
a circle	51
letter from a youth to his prospective employer	52
north hill road, leeds	53
new year '75, leeds	54
evening	55
accelerando	56
commonplace	57
& the tide	58
there is no future in nostalgia	59
an afternoon nap	60
the coffee house, cockpit hotel	61
similes	62
dawn	63
absolute	64
another look	65
dracula	66
things	67
configuration	68
group dynamics I	69
group dynamics II	70

from *Down The Line* (1980)

they are days	73
paper	74
shipwreck	75
medium	76
down the line	77
night scene I	80
night scene II	81
would it have been	82
a lesson on the definite article	83
the grammar of a dinner	84
event	85
roll call	86
samson & delilah	87
rsvp regrets only	88
in memory of) anthony	89
for...	90
until	91
words	92
postlude	93
mime	94
late-night bonus	95
traffic	96
most of october	97
sights	98
at balmain	99
i think (a book of changes)	100
2 mothers in a h d b playground	101
fiscal ear	103

from *Man Snake Apple* (1986)

tropical paradise	107
stained glass	108
still-life I	109
still-life IV	110
still-life V	111
still-life VI	112
man snake apple	113

your goodness	116
dialogue	117
in the quiet of the night	118
when last seen	119
dinosaurs	120
street scene I	121
street scene II	122
foursome	123
exchanges	125
alternation	125
eyes	127
nightjar	128
paraphrase	129
a good poem	130
the shisen-do	131
12-times table	132
at nagoya	133
i can't remember where	134
a peony display, ueno park	135
i am not sure	136
a list of things	137
paired stills	138
waterbabies	140
denpasar	142
cianjur	143
Notes	145

Introduction

Arthur Yap is a poet of everyday life. Everyday life is one of repetition in which the replicability of our life functions is encoded in the replicability of every day. It is also the framework in which those life functions come to be organised within the sphere of the social. In the strategies and practices of everyday life, therefore, we see the interplay of the individual and society. Everyday life can be seen, therefore, as representative of communal and even national experience. This latter case is especially true of a small island state like Singapore. Singapore's national culture, then, can be described in terms of the everyday, as Chua Beng Huat suggests:

> If I am to talk about the Singaporean culture, then really it's the common transformation of everyday life that is important ... If there is a Singapore national culture, we should increasingly begin to talk about [it in terms of] that commonality.

Yap's interest in the everyday is apparent throughout his four volumes of poetry. In *Only Lines*, for example, the poem, 'it rains today', announces Yap's interest in everyday life. The scene is an urban one, framed - as a number of scenes in Yap's *oeuvre* - by a window; nature is depicted in its interface with culture and the way that it is tailored within the public spaces of the city. In this sense his poetry diverges from the project of romanticism in that more often than not nature is depicted as domesticated and urbanised - part of the landscape of everyday life rather than as belonging to a sublime, spiritual or transcendental landscape.

In 'it rains today' the poet observes the everyday event of rain. We are told that this is one of many rainy days, but that on this occasion the poet views the scene differently. The poet first establishes a sense of repetition: 'the trees are wet today' is followed by 'the child is wet with rain today'. The repetition of the word 'rain' - introduced in the title - creates both a sense of the pervasive, monotonous downpour and also of rain as a repetitious act, one that has happened frequently (see for example the repetition of 'every rain' in the second stanza) and thus has established a strong sense of familiarity for the poet.

As I have suggested, this poem describes the familiar event of the rain but here the rain is a repetition with a slight variation: although the poem revolves around the familiar and unadorned images of trees, child and rain, the poet states: 'until this rain / i've never found / trees child and rain / so precisely'. He imagines or pictures this particular familiar scene more 'precisely' than before. This precision is brought about through the effect of defamiliarisation. The images present themselves to the poet as 'a little shift / either side of reality'. In other words our familiar sense of reality is 'shifted' and the trees, child and rain are viewed differently, that is, more vividly or 'precisely'. We can see here that Yap is a poet of the mundane, the banal and the small familiar details of everyday life, and that the mundane and the familiar are made fresh and new in the poetry. This is not to say that they are translated into the realm of the mythic or symbolic. They remain firmly anchored in the realm of the quotidian, that is, of repetition and mundanity.

Everyday life is thus not depicted as an impoverished realm to be transformed or translated in moments of epiphany and insight into a higher transcendent level of awareness. Everyday life is not contemptible or boring, according to Yap; it is the means by which we know ourselves in the world. By looking at the parts, the structure and the composition of the ways in which we know the everyday world, especially their visual and verbal aspects, Yap invites us to see the remarkable continuity and productivity of daily life and to take pleasure in this (re)cognition.

Everyday life is repetitious (that is, 'perpetual', as the poem of that title suggests and 'daily' as we see in the poem 'new year') and Yap's project of exploring the everyday uses language in specific ways. He generally avoids the use of metaphor, symbolism and allegory. This is not to say that he never uses these tropes (as we see later, for example, in some of the poems in *Down The Line* and *Man Snake Apple*) but that he often uses imagery in a literal and flat way; the imagery of trees, rain and child, as for example, in 'it rains today', does not invite a metaphoric, allegoric or symbolic reading.

The tropes he makes most use of are those of parallelism and parataxis. He repeats, reiterates and paraphrases so that the poems develop through a layering effect. In this event closure becomes problematic. In the poem 'location', for example, which describes a village in which bicycles are continually arriving and departing, the poem closes with the image of a bicycle dropped on the grass, a stationary moment in the perpetual cycle of change; the bike, Yap says, 'is just resting / sufficiently / to make no sense at all'. This inconclusiveness, this moment outside utility, explanation or narrative, does not present us with closure of the conventional kind. We have instead a kind of opening out, an expansive ending that in effect leads us back into the poem, into the image of bikes arriving and departing and the cycles (my pun is intended) of movement and change which, in this poem as in many others, invoke the spectre of modernity and industrialisation.

The theme of the transformation of a rural culture into an urbanised, industrial one appears briefly throughout *only lines* in other poems such as 'expansion' and 'coming up, flowers'. In many of these poems there is certainly a hint of nostalgia for a way of life (like that, for example, portrayed in 'location') that is passing. However, Yap's nostalgia, even in *Only Lines* where it is most prominent, never becomes maudlin or excessive. The traces of nostalgia we see in *Only Lines* appear even more fleetingly in *Commonplace* where Yap comes to the conclusion that 'there is no future in nostalgia'. There is a sense of acceptance and almost of resignation in the face of change although not an uncritical, unquestioning or unequivocal acceptance nor the suggestion that the past can or should be forgotten.

Yap as a poet is much interested in the past and in memory. In 'location', for example, the village becomes a potent emblem of the persistence of memory in an industrialised age; memory affirms continuity and perpetuity in a changing environment. Memory seems at times to be at odds with the nationalist discourse of economic development which strives to create linear narratives of progression and sequentiality in contrast with the repetitive nature of memory. The latter gives rise to the tropes of parataxis and parallelism which evoke the aggregative, additive and iterative nature of memory which, unlike history or nationalism, does not always order events in relative and (con)sequential association implying a linear and causative progression of events and ideas.

Memory often relates in a cyclic way to the past (re)establishing continuities that exist outside history. The repetitive, layered syntax of the first stanza in 'location' - 'if i stay here any longer / i am already / where i shall always be' - adeptly enacts the paradox of memory: that one exists in the past and the present simultaneously and that one's future will always be conditioned by and predicated upon one's past. In this sense one is always 'located' in the past. Conversely, of course, the past is continually 'rewritten' by the present and the images of former times, glimpses of village life and peranakan culture, are conjured up in Yap's poetry within the context of the transfigured contemporary world. It has been suggested that postmodernity is characterised by amnesia and forgetting; hence our fascination with museums and notions of heritage which fabricate a past. However, in communities such as Singapore, where modernity has brought transmogrifying cultural change within the space of a generation, memory is constantly activated by the striking polarity of the colonial past and the contemporary industrialised nation-state and the brief span of time in which this transformation has been enacted.

'old house at ang siang hill' further explores ideas of the past and of memory. The lines, 'an unusual house this is / dreams are here before you sleep', suggest the persistence of the past and of memory in the present; the present is in effect a 'dream' that re-enacts the past. The poem points to the precariousness of the past in a rapidly modernising country; the old house has already become a 'house-that-was' in the face of 're-development'. The poem suggests, however, that although the past apparently leaves no 'ghosts' (we are told: 'so what if this is / your grandfather's house / his ghost doesn't live here anymore'), it is nonetheless haunted by an awareness of 'tradition' and a sense of loss; 'nothing much will be missed / eyes not tradition tell you this'. Memory, by nourishing and deepening the present through a sense of tradition, simultaneously reminds us of the things lost to us. The poem suggests that we are beings precariously placed in a modernised urban landscape which, although it has almost no visible trace of the past (our 'eyes' will uncover nothing of the past), is nonetheless saturated with the memory of that invisible past and with the loss experienced in the wake of change. In this ghostly landscape the present is, in effect, a waking 'dream'; we inhabit two realities simultaneously, the world of the present and the memory of a lifestyle now gone.

This scenario has intriguing implications in the context of Singapore's troubled relationship with modernity, capitalism and democracy, discourses it has inherited from the West and stages locally in an ambivalent nationalist discourse of resistance and participation. While the notion of economic development occupies centre stage in Singaporean nationalism, the notion of traditional 'Asian' values, for example, drawn from the cultures of origin of Singapore's multiracial population, constitutes a discourse of heritage, origins and authenticity, which is mobilised as a resistance to those aspects of the western discourses which are seen as undesirable. In other words the pre-colonial past, which has been largely eclipsed in the race for development, is reinvented along specific and tailored lines in order to manage the contemporary hybrid postcolonial culture.

Yap's second volume, *Commonplace* (1977), continues an exploration of many of the issues apparent in *Only Lines*. The titular poem elaborates his continuing interest in everyday life. The repetition of everyday life, the poet suggests, is a creative and inventive experience of renewal: 'everything has happened before / but there is nothing to compare it / each time, with each time that it recurs'. The paradoxical doubling over of the syntax in the last line here invokes the almost hypnotic effect of repetition. Although these repetitions take place within a larger fixed structure - that of the everyday or, to be specific, in this case the everyday work life of the citizens - at the moment of their enactment they are corporeal events with material value and pleasure. The poem evokes the clockwork demarcation and repetition of the work day including the routine breakfast rush, lethargic afternoons and peak hour traffic at the end of the day. The staging of everyday life in this way lends it a dramatic and visual quality (for example, the movement of shadows across the city) and in this sense is a celebration of the everyday and the commonplace.

The everyday is dramatised through a series of defamiliarised images which mark the passing of the hours: 'two stained blobs on a clear canvas', 'three fingers tapping a tattoo on the table', 'three upward gulls'. This defamiliarisation makes us see the day through a different lens and to see it as a different set of events. This changed way of seeing is echoed in the last four lines of the poem. Having made the comment 'when night comes, it will come in neonlights', the poet rephrases it as a question: 'when night comes, will it come in darkness / or will it bring its own light to a well-scrubbed day?' The interrogative mood invokes a change of perception, a means of apprehending reality differently - literally through a process of questioning - just as the night brings 'its own light', its own way of seeing, to the scene that was formerly 'a well-scrubbed day'. What we have here, in the words of the poem 'only lines', is 'the same old story', but told differently, that is, told anew. The significance lies in the repetition with variation; the living and the telling of each new day is enacted through the same routines and the same language but with variation.

'commonplace' ends with the line 'will there be any doubt that commonplace is?' The answer to this is, yes, momentarily, through the process of defamiliarisation. However, defamiliarisation does not remove the quotidian from the realm of the commonplace by transporting it into a mythic realm; the poet insists: 'i should never whip the commonplace / for the meaning of its opposite'. Rather, the poem investigates an aesthetics of the everyday and suggests that language itself, in its common and colloquial usage, is as complex and multi-faceted as are the routine events of the everyday. Yap not only defamiliarises the imagery and pattern of the work day but also our expectations of language; the lyrical poetics of romanticism are replaced with a flat and literal language which constantly doubles back on itself making the reader aware momentarily of the intricate and invisible and minute workings of language by which we make meaning of the everyday world.

That Yap is interested particularly in the discursive structures of language and knowledge we can see in his fascination with the notion of frames. I've already mentioned that many of his scenes are framed by a window; in two other poems from *Commonplace*, 'everything's coming up numbers' and 'another look', he examines numerical categories and the framing discourses of art ('an explanation, an appraisal / a catalogue listing') respectively. In the poem, 'things', the action is viewed again through a window. This image of framing is followed up by casting the imagined scenario of the poem as a film; this dramatic device suggests that the everyday is the stage for our life dramas, be they joyful or tragic. Our dreams and our demons are not portrayed as 'other' to the mundanity of everyday life but as part and parcel of it.

There is, moreover, in 'things' an emphasis on surfaces - as if everyday objects and events are the arena of our dramas - rather than an invocation of hidden and metaphorical depths in order to portray emotionality. (This is not to argue that the poetry's language is non-figurative; the colloquial phrase 'hung up', for example, is punned upon in a very resonant way.) The 'things' or objects in movies, as in our 'dreams', are 'imperfect realia', once-removed, as Plato suggests, from reality. Words, also, could be considered 'imperfect realia' and language, in the context of this poem, a form of dreaming. The desk is the site of dreaming and of language in the poem, and the other everyday 'things' listed at the beginning of the poem - 'chair', 'wall', 'window' and 'bed' - are domestic, everyday objects which set the scene of the drama. Just as these 'things' are everyday objects, so too are words; they are used day after day, often in repetitive and commonplace ways. The list of everyday objects at the beginning of the poem presents these images in an unadorned and non-lyrical way which militates against their investment with any high-art literary aura. The list effect, along with Yap's penchant for lower-case letters, affirms that his poetics focus on the field of the everyday usage of colloquial language rather than that of high art and the romantic discourse of heightened emotion. Everyday life, however apparently undramatic, Yap suggests, is the stage upon which our hopes and fears are played out in whatever form.

Yap's third book, *Down The Line* (1980), is perhaps his most substantial, not from the point of view of volume but of the project he undertakes. There are a number of longer poems and poem sequences in this book which explore the glamour and achievement of the rapidly modernised and industrialised city-state and also such complex issues as high-density living in Singapore, the extent and reach of governmental social engineering and government intervention in the everyday life of its citizens. In many ways this book can been seen as a reflection and a record of the 1970s. If Benedict Anderson defined the nation as an imagined community whose members never actually meet each other, Singapore, being a small island of high-density living, is a nation where this dictum comes closest to being challenged. As a city-state, where a large number of people live in close proximity, there is a visual awareness of the community's boundedness and of the geographical demarcation of the nation.

The poems of *Down The Line* focus on the experience of city living. In the poem 'shipwreck' the poet explores the fantasy and the marvel that a 'splendid shipwreck' inspires in childhood: 'my pen raced. at that age / i chased themes that were totally mine'. This unrestrained enthusiasm is contrasted with the reduction in imagination that comes with a formal education and a scientific and financial assessment of the same phenomenon. In an inventive visual sleight of hand the poet compares the marvellous shipwreck with the city of Singapore:

a shipwreck is a tall shore of humanity.
with an island background, it had been composed

on sand, dry inland, crafted by hand.
it can be seen in the city, daily,
neatly.

The last two lines suggest a similar reduction of the imagination and a shift from the original inspired vision of something 'splendid' to the management of a city which is orderly and 'neat'.

Yap's interest in the city is further elaborated in the poem sequence 'dramatis personae' which explores the public spaces of the city, specifically those constructed for leisure and recreation. These public spaces - the public park, public beach and public pond - are anomalous and liminal spaces in that they are areas where nature and the city meet and overlap. Nature appears both in its 'natural' form (the beach) and in its urbanised and domesticated forms (the park and the pond). The liminality of these spaces is foregrounded by the rhetorical question, 'where does the road end & the beach begin?', the interrogative mood of which highlights the uncertainty of this border zone. The people who visit these recreational areas exhibit a similarly uncertain identity; they are described oxymoronically as 'young men & women, old boys & girls'. The juxtaposition of 'young' with 'men' and 'women', and of 'old' with 'boys' and 'girls', suggests some contradictions in the roles and identities the people assume; there is some slippage between the available conventional categories. However, this failure is not seen as pathological or invidious; perhaps it is 'normal' in that many people occasionally find themselves in the margins of conventionality. The poet is non-judgemental and accepting in his portrait of the citizenry who are seen as complex and vulnerable: 'how we laugh & then cry, / since we bring you some happiness / you should also have some of our sadness'.

The title of the poem evokes the allegory of the theatre. The poem seems to suggest that there is a kind of corporeal renewal enacted in public rituals of recreation and leisure. It's not a question here of private individuals versus public places, but of people 'acting out' their everyday lives (the title 'dramatis personae' foregrounds the notion of performance) in both private and public places; and in the theatre of everyday life we observe the interdependency of person and society. These are poems, in fact, about being citizens. Public and private realms are mediated by the citizen in the course of everyday life. There is a sense of pleasure in the actions of the dramatis personae, that is, the corporeal pleasure of the repetition and ritual of everyday life. In the imagery of the poems there is also a sense of poignancy at the loss of certain small freedoms; the flowers in the park are not to be picked: 'they are for the public'; the landcrabs 'webbed', 'sewn' and 'trapped' by their cement environment are a telling metaphor; and the little boys' carefree play among the weeds is contrasted with 'the lesson/on fish & waterlife & diagrams' that they must endure elsewhere.

The free-spirited play of the children, contrasted with their formal education, is reminiscent of the theme of the 'shipwreck'. 'dramatis personae' seems to go one step further in suggesting that renewal is possible within everyday life and the public spaces of the city. The theatrical allegory takes on spiritual overtones at the end of the poem in the image of ritualistic rebirth where the children's faces, reflected in the surface of the pond, are like 'terrible fish' rising to the surface; out of the 'week's gloom' and the 'old familiarity' there appears 'each sunday' a renewal of the anomalous and the unexpected in the midst of the everyday.

The poem sequence that follows 'dramatis personae', 'down the line', opens as a celebration of the visual spectacle and life energy of the city. This collective life energy, the poem suggests, will always be in excess of systems of classification, monitoring and control; the city, the poet says, 'is liquid graphics, / neither statistics nor logistics can propel'. It will also be in excess of homogenising and totalising discourses as 'every part, every space [is] / larger & more real than the entirety'. We see a similar celebration of the multifariousness and activity of the city in another poem, 'traffic', where the city is described as 'a connection of many things / that cannot undergo any physical editing'. The city, however, for all its visual magnificence, is also a place of work. The notion of everyday labour is evoked in the image of crabs (an image we also see in 'dramatis personae'), labouring on the beach where they

> lay at the water's edge a library of margins.
> page by page, it prefabricates the day's
> ins & outs but, like pure callisthenics,
> seem never quite enough.

The repetition of daily work here is described as 'pure callisthenics' and the nation is seen as the site of discipline. The concepts of labour and hard work and also of discipline and control are juxtaposed with the beauty and also the imagination of the city-state. The manual labourers, for example, are 'without speech'. In the second and fourth sections the poem develops a pointed critique of the officialese of social engineering, the propaganda of official nationalism: 'what everyone will tell you is what everyone / wants to hear, has been told'; 'credulity is a bigger commodity than credibility'. Yap describes the continual saturation with propaganda as 'a battery of ear-assault'. The poem depicts the extensive transformation of the everyday lives of the people, a process brought about through the rapid modernisation of the city-state. In evoking the reach of government propaganda and the extent to which government planning and the dictates of economic development affect every aspect of people's everyday lives, the poem is a sustained critique of the intervention of the state in civil society and the private lives of its citizens. It points to the conflation of state and civil society and the shrinking of the private sphere.

What we see in these poems from *Down The Line* is a vernacular and informal sense of history. They convey a clear sense of the Singaporean people as having a national history, and of the nation as the product of a great deal of labour, effort, discipline and sacrifice. In 'down the line' Yap critiques the totalising discourse of official nationalism; what we can see as an alternative in these poems, I suggest, is a kind of grass-roots nationalism: informal bonding which takes place at the local level. A people's and a nation's informal sense of history is based on memory, and memory is local before it can be national.

If these are poems that epitomise citizenship, they are poems, moreover, that bear the trace of nostalgia. (As I have suggested, Yap's first two volumes are more strongly marked by nostalgia which, although it decreases in intensity, is still evident in the last two volumes). Nostalgia is not rebellion - these citizens accept their lot - but it is subversive of official constructions of history. Memory and history are processes by which we negotiate the relation of the past to the present in our everyday lives. To engage actively with the past in the present is to live in and with a sense of loss. Where the official nationalism of a modernising nation by necessity plays down the price paid for progress, this price lives on in the memory of its citizens, and is evident in the sense of resignation, acceptance, and endurance that is characteristic of Yap's poetry in the 1970s.

Man Snake Apple (1986), Yap's fourth book, develops the allegorical elements we have seen in *Down The Line*. While many of the poems in this volume are characterised by a playful use of language and an essentially non-lyrical prosaic style often marked by a tendency to the epigrammatic and the cryptic - features also characteristic of his earlier work - the titular sequence is an ambitious, complex, far-ranging and sustained allegory of late-capitalist consumerism. The biblical story of the Creation is transformed into a postmodern fable which explores the trajectories of desire and knowledge through modernity. The dense, convoluted language with its ornate, rococo figurings of repetition, parallelism, parataxis, oxymoron, paradox, irony, symbolism, ambiguity, hyperbole, contradiction and double-entendre, and its disrupted syntax, multi-syllabic words, double-barrelled nouns and adjectives and hybird generic constructions creates a sense of excess and superfluity. The storytelling narrative voice orchestrates this voluptuous excess with a long, prosaic, rhythmic line which creates a spellbinding, hypnotic effect. The story that entrances us is an allegory of fascination, appetite, desire and the will to knowledge unfolding in the anticipatory rhetoric and tension of the language. Given its interest in desire, pleasure and consumerism, and the fact that the body is the arena in which these are appetites are played out, this poetic sequence could be described as *écriture féminine* - a text which 'writes the body', a history of the (male) body in the arena of modernity and the global flows of trans-national capital.

The prayer-like ending of the sequence invokes both a sense of closure and of cyclic repetition; it also links the poem to other themes in the book such as that introduced in the opening poem - 'tropical paradise' - of the seasonal cycles of fecundity and death. Images of paradise and abundance are juxtaposed in this poem with those of meditative silence and an almost ascetic poise and stillness. This latter mood is reflected in some of the 'still-life' studies that follow; the Japanese poems towards the end of the book are also characterised by the paradox of fecundity and asceticism in 'tropical paradise'. This sense of paradox is further explored in the context of language. The language of 'man snake apple' and some of the later Japanese poems is characterised by an abundance of detail and figurative play as I have suggested, and Yap brings our attention to the polysemous, ambiguous and playful nature of language that poetry exploits, in two poems about language, 'alternation' and 'paraphrase'. In the latter poem he describes the way language takes on a life of its own: 'the word swallows the world', he suggests; 'the word comes close to carrying its own ontology, / its own reward for being'. And the poem 'alternation' provides us with a coda to the reading of Yap's *oeuvre* and the conundrums it so often presents to the reader: 'there isn't a single, disappointing, unchanging answer'.

Arthur Yap's prize-winning volumes of poetry span twenty years or so of contemporary Singaporean life and articulate, as I've suggested, a vernacular and informal sense of that nation's history through its portraiture of the everyday life of the city-state. In 'still-life v' (*Man Snake Apple*) he returns to one of his favourite subjects, the park pond, where 'nothing is happening, / a non-event at no time recorded for posterity'. The paradoxically full and empty moments of everyday life are the repository of collective memory and the arena in which local bonding and interdependency of the individual and society is played out. Walter Benjamin has said that 'the past can be seized only as an image which flashes up at the instant when it can be recognised and is never seen again'. *The Space Of City Trees* captures these flashes of everyday life and allows us many repeated moments of recognition.

Anne Brewster
Curtin University

from
ONLY LINES
[1971]

to my parents

only lines

should i also add:
here are only lines
linked by the same old story.
the same basic plot
in which they are grown

should add
little doubt the field is only green
the sky the same old blue
in the presence of my eyes,
your preference
(though not mine)
should see for your own eyes
and if you can laugh
care with some concern
it is because (like me)
you need lines
to add up this same old story

location

so this village is still here
here without change
and if i stay here any longer
i am already
where i shall always be
here without change

in this village still here.
some things remain
some things pass,
some things are tired
bicycles arriving
cleaned bicycles departing.
and if today
not many people are arriving
do not change the day
to bring in yesterday
riding an old identity
which, anywhere,
has come and gone
every year ago.
and if you see a bicycle
leaning on the grass
neither tired nor cleaned
then it is just resting
sufficiently
to make no sense at all

sunny day

sunny day
comes through the window
and sits on the table.

sunny day,
he chose to be killed
diaphragm against steering wheel
for the car seemed newer
the senses keener.
only the road was closer.

sunny day licks up paint
on the window-sill
and the heart, grown cooler,
(only the skin is warmer)
sees withering flowers
offered to him on the hill

and it is isolation

hurrying ahead

there was a large house up the road.
it is a small house
and mainly dead,
those living are moving out.

the road is like a snake
running a slow quarter mile,
needs shaping round the bend
to drain the rain easily.
the grass is past green
when a drought is on,
those leaving have to hurry
before the grass returns
to green for an eternity
and reality becomes more mixed
than is imagined.
then it is not so bad
for another eternity.
those moving are not just going
they are hurrying ahead
when the grass is dying
before they are also dying
dying a few steps after the grass
where they had come to live
not die
nor ask
why any grass should die

one road

the road northwards
ended at ch'ah
on a fine april morning,
here the car broke down
and the sun followed us
in a bus to segamat.

next morning
the road continued
under a repaired car.
glad were we to feel the breeze
hear the roar of other engines,
having ended a night's hotel discomfort
here were both open road
and prospect of city:
the sum of what's not small town.
it was here, at gemas,
it was here at tampin
we wondered if we hadn't passed
this way yesterday
for at any four o'clock
children were pyjama-clad.

if we can be sure
that the road running hundreds of miles
would not bring along its periphery,
that here and there
when it is twelve o'clock
the sun has not risen nor set

then everything else could well wait

panchor

year by year
wood returns to ashes
and also as trees and flowers.
some grow some bloom
some wither and some rally
in support of others
as they climb and climb
to reach for the sun
splintering its light on the ground
touching the soil with life,
flow up as sap
bursting in green leaves
on branches of the wild rambutan.

squat under, the sultan's monument
is seen and appraised.
hands reached out
spanning the years
to pluck the rambutans
the sultan had never eaten,
throw the shells down river
where there was a ton of gold.

a little later
the boat pulled from the jetty,
there was a lull
and then the landscape settled down.

garden episode

in the garden two children
set fire to their sparklers
and it wasn't a festival.
the boy drew a coloured circle
showing the amah in the dark
perched on a little stool
and she was here a long time ago.
jubilant, the little girl's brand
trailed over a bush
with a shatter of light
quickly over
as they walked to the house:
"you're a big boy now, too heavy to carry".
she stooped over the puny child, barely five,
lifting him from under the arms
and trotted, fat, with the neglected girl
clinging to her samfoo.
her smile was like that, thirty years back,
of a slim woman vacant over her dead child;

while pulling each gently by the ear
to their bedtime, she had forgotten
that a few more years would make her
think of the night with little stars
as she grows punitive over two children
not weary from sums and rounders
scattering her thoughts freely as they come

expansion

no stretch of darkened sky
would show a patch of red
a patch of sunset.

where the sun will not stay
after dark
the skyline of houses
grows with the sky
and who can tell
what is this completion;
i cannot chew the month to days
masticate the day to hours
and line the hours each to each
saying, out of context, i die.
where once a single day
was a day and a night
it is now the amoeba of day
of night,
the line of sponge houses
soaks in the sky
as the sponge sky
seeps into the houses.
where once houses hung from sky
they now are clutches.
so one urban expansion
has to lean on another
or they die

while the tree of night grows and grows

coming up, flowers

coming up, flowers.
and just how long
will it take to have all re-arranged?

fields sprawl in midday sun,
i must've been mad
to think i could live
with bricks and concrete
when, all the while,
the rurality pitched over
all its dung
wearing fields like badges.
growing flowers in batches
was the only bunch
of brickbats i've had.

flowers change with the months,
i wonder when it's my turn
to receive (your accolades)
but there's still the problem
of what happens when they're dead

perpetual

sit and watch this woman
in every house she hangs
curtains in every room,
takes out a pile of washing
to spread dry on every line.
every nearby baby perking in the sun
turns sweaty, cries hopefully
for another cake, another nipple.
every woman shouts in anger
does not anyway always whisper
does not at all read the papers

cares not for the moon's soft light
that erases every baby in sleep.
and every woman now is stalking
through all the days following

old photographs

mainly, they're old photographs,
my standing here, your standing there.

when my sister wrote from london
of hippies loitering along the streets
i've also seen them everywhere,
in Life and Time they appear
and it's difficult to tell if they loiter.

i must've seen in the flesh
people in memorable situations
either of success or failure,
only it cannot be claimed
such images are perpetual.
in newspapers they're more real
more decisive in their happiness or sorrow.

and, there, they're the oldest photographs.
it is that no one has changed

precedence

well into november, there hasn't been
the start of the monsoon.
voices have not preceded owners
helping themselves over puddles.
in a few days, likely
the sky will tremble with stored storms
that seen across the window will be
rain hanging over the road, not gentle
nor grating. it is a constant seeping
and a wind pushes it to new shapes
of landscape.

this evening it is raining stars
all the more clearly,
there is no spangling moon

it rains today

the trees are wet with rain today
a child holds an umbrella
walking over grass.
very quickly
a wind lifts his umbrella
the child is wet with rain today,

the trees in front of him
exist for every rain
and every rain
outside my window
comes before my gaze,
becomes this familiarity
i always see.
rain after rain
until this rain
i've never found
trees child and rain
so precisely
a little shift
either side of reality

old house at ang siang hill

an unusual house this is
dreams are here before you sleep
tread softly
into the three-storeyed gloom
sit gently
on the straits-born furniture
imported from china
speak quietly
to the contemporary occupants

they are not afraid of you
waiting for you to go
before they dislocate your intentions
so what if this is
your grandfather's house
his ghost doesn't live here anymore
your family past is
superannuated grime
which increases with time
otherwise nothing adds or subtracts
the bricks and tiles
until re-development
which will greatly change
this house-that-was
dozens like it along the street
the next and the next as well

nothing much will be missed
eyes not tradition tell you this

in passing

yesterday you were in k.l., the day before you
were somewhere else; now, you are here
trying out our telephone-lines and the air-
conditioning system, saying that our system is
more adequate than that in new york where you
come from. but you are so tired of running and we,
not having run, drove you to the seaside restaurant
feted you on the speciality of chilli-crabs and fried
noodles to which you said: it's so unlike the
spaghetti i had in italy.

you brought, from a friend, an l.p. for us to share
with regards. you exclaimed in chinatown that it
was all so intriguing while we, not wanting to
be perfunctory, left you to your intrigue. then
at the airport, with its mural, its coffee, we
waited, while talking and talking, for you to comment
on the fine building, the mural assembling the sea-
front or, even, the air-conditioning.

but you were fumbling your bag for your sweater

readjustment

after being educationally years away
he returned
expecting us to have remained ourselves.
we expected the mod suit
which he wore
and only that didn't belong here
(otherwise he was himself).

we'll listen to his talk
show concern, create some problems
offer our solutions
to prevent the rise of questions
which might need readjustment.
and only these do not belong here.

when it happens
we cannot cover
our consoling smiles
or smile to ourselves
that we are not torn
between a family and another country
then we know
we can't just go away
and drop our faces
to bridge the span
between our eyes and his heart

change of pace

today the sun tumbles out
scattering its spectrum wetly over grass
rushing children to play
on their weekly saturday.
the sun wears its fast 6 o'clock slant
and after today — who can say?

see how people change.

tomorrow there may be rain
pencilling briskly down
and the spectrum scattering.
what can we say
when the sun wears a 6 o'clock slant?

see now, people run

sunday

let me be glad if i see my thoughts
hang a mosquito-net over my head
burying me from inquiring existence:
the four corners one reliquary
till morning.
i should toss the net over my head
come out with one sudden thought:
how little ground i'll cover
to emerge to breakfast.

but this is sunday
without need to ask for knowledge
to found worlds
words to trigger profundity:
i hear my voice finding a thought
but do not question
create no simple guile
let me just lie
watching the day
with the morning
                    opening my window-sill

a scroll painting

the mountains are hazy with timeless passivity
sprawling monotonously in the left-hand corner
while clouds diffuse and fill the entire top half
before bumping daintily into a bright red parakeet
perched suicide-like on a beautifully gnarled branch
arched by the weight of fruit and one ripe peach
hung a motionless inch from the gaping beak

here is transient beauty
caught in permanence
but of what avail is such perpetual unattainment?

i know the stupid bird can never eat the stupid peach

cameron highlands

1. the road leads
not to clouds in the sky
only mists in a race
vying in ability to merge
as one fluid whole distinguished
by shades of purple-grey

on one side
the cliffs are 100 feet drops

2. at the end of this road
beyond cabbages and farms
let me think ahead,
but not too much
i know i cannot ring
like an alarm clock

3. it is here that a person
becomes a bare statement,
nothing seems very real
except what lies ahead unseen

balancing sounds

(not unusual) but early
brinchang rekindles activity
a 9 p.m. prelude
to the town's deep sleep
not many minutes later

silence walks down the road
under a bright patch of cloud
nesting in tall treetops
and a star hangs not far
picking faintly out
the white roadline
left side you are

coming back
to tanah rata,
hear its output of dogs
bark away the silence so far
so close, retreating
up again the misty road
shivering 4 miles back to brinchang

seasonal

soft-pawing the sky
are splayed leaves,
otherwise they're falling down:

ancient wind

swells this garden like a balloon
every minute blown larger
until it's about to burst:

ancient season
fascinates. we can't take
our eyes away
though it is not quite there

every casualty is happy
mindless in an abstract way
tracing where the wind ends
and it is right here
(we're the aftermath next month).
where it began, we were there:
ancient monsoon

from

FIVE TAKES

[1974]

(with 4 other poets)

dramatis personae

i. public park

along the bench we're variations of a line
that watch the many flowers grow
into our understanding, and die
because we are not to pick them.
they are for the public,
we in public are private figures
humanising the landscape
on the little hill. under the trees
we listen for the millennium
while following the turn of the floral clock
with the knock of a new plastic heart.
this part is self-centred
it takes and it rejects.

this park is self-centred
and outsiders just get in the way.
today you are in the park
waiting for us, watching us
young men and women, old boys and girls,
parking ourselves. (how we laugh).
how we laugh and then cry,
since we bring you some happiness
you should also have some of our sadness

ii. public beach

where does the road end and the beach begin?
it is not easy to say, so closely
do the two forms intermingle
blending the neat sharp smell of petrol
with the warm scent of dirty sand.

here is the sand,
and further from the sand

(can you see?)
here is the sea.
sand and sea are less today
as there is more of life.

webbed up here by the sewer
sewn to the hardness of cement
trapped by piss-moss, little landcrabs
are more crust than crab and salt.
and caught here, we would never have been
more than all these things we have seen.
that cemented here, as we are not,
we run away before the waves arrive
with a little last fresh collapse

iii.   public pond

coming down to the very bank
the soil is very old and crumbly.
you would not laugh
seeing it so, for it is yours.
today you are a pond, a still pond
hoping for the little boys to happen
there with their jars, here with their nets.
they drown
because you are too abstract
when they bend over you
searching among weeds for what they want
before they turn to conceits, the lesson
on fish and waterlife and diagrams,
with no waterdrops of agitation on their hands.

it is important they come each sunday
replacing the week's gloom with their faces.
in you they drown, an old familarity,
and they will rise again day after day
after this, like some terrible fish.
for their simplicity is your certainty

statement

of course your work comes first.
after that, you may go for a walk,
visit friends but, all the same,
it is always correct to ask
before you do anything else.

so if you say: please may i jump
off the ledge? and go on to add
this work is really killing,
you will be told: start jumping.
no one is in any way
narrow-minded anymore these days.
it is that everyone likes to know
these things way beforehand.
but if you state: i'm going now,
jumping off the ledge
most probably they will say nothing,
thinking should it legally, morally,
departmentally be yes/no/perhaps,
or if it's not too late:
why don't you come along? we shall bring
this matter up to a higher level

fire off kim seng bridge

a burning sun
as i watch
clatters on the bridge

scattering black butterflies in the breeze.
burning huts throw pale flames in the heat.
drawing so much anodic space
huts and people seem to nudge
towards the centre of the heap.
smoke seams the scene
in a sheet of silence.

and so what are world crises,
spearheads of unrest so prevalent?
in this silent fear
the rest becomes conditional,
and things being coeval
you could walk out and get killed.
it makes so little difference

the send-off

even as children are chanting fascinations
about new year, we mythologise the act and fact
of its passing. passing, the opening of the year
wears its traditional accessories, with red
to balance in the ecology of superstition.

the year that is past
substituted its time and movement for yours
and took you away from nothing
not already familiar, asked nothing
not already dispensible.
a year has no revelations,
it must come and go
making some older, some younger by their absence.
a year conceals, does not reveal
meanings, portents or omens.
it springs with the tiger, sneaks in with the rat
and if it is not wet, a dry year cherishes itself
sunning the tower-block and the hut.
old griefs, new hopes
all become their own revelations
as the city sleeps, is tired from the weight
of responsibility that is time's endowment

these sounds, endlessly

these sounds, endlessly. ears were had.
it wouldn't have been bad had they
been of leaves falling. instead, they were many things
going away: harsh grating removal noises
incessantly, heaving the house inside out.

inside out,
the new house is a few new sounds.
when these fail, ears are had.
it is sad to add that when ears fail
eyes are also had
by a little graphic failure
(true to scale,
very dear
the ways things go).

going, feet are gone.
so let there be not too much hurry,
there is nothing that does not need move
away. any way
you see it
you are there, had, (too bad).

almost still-life

it was easy to become a stranger.
having walked into every room,
all rooms were empty.
i wondered if what troubled me

was not this house, this old man
whose window-ears have been constantly washed
by laughter and shouts of anger;
whose tattered shutter-eyes
(both precise and obscured)
have focused upon a paradox
and drawn it right up to the knees, its stairs,
so as not to show its heart empty.

the old house was like a shell
and seemed to have wrapped
emptiness up as a parcel.
i could not see its eyes clearly
enough to know if, at midnight, the ghosts
would come and retrieve the gifts
of bricks and concrete and fingers

recurrent imagery

just as the tree which seems caught
a little ahead of an idiomatic sunrise
is but an image,
so is the student reading his thoughts into a book,
the painter and his paints,
and the woman nursing her newborn child
who looks like a little old man.

sun rising, the tree is not the same.
the child is fresh and fairly recent.
and every few years bring on differences
which, differently asked and answered,
are conceit to conceit
variously the same.

you do not think these are images.
sun and child start all over again
watching you watch them take away
colours from the face which had been yours,
and all you need is bring the tree to sun
itself in the corridor you have lined with your years

minimum excavation

poised like a large settlement
of raw minerals at ground level
they are also for excavation,
these feelings of uncertainty.
pared to a minimum
the answer is
yes or no.

no intricate adornment
of fernroots, young shoots,
detract the hard and cold.
busy hands shift terrains,
lay down a horizon
dividing nothing
more than itself

which is finite enough in its suggestion
that long-ago memories
are now exposed, posing
for the benefit of stony spectators

banyan tree

showers catching the intersect
of this road and the next
grow the tree greener than paint.
its roots though themselves nothing
siphon in spreading air
pluck birds from the sky
to rest within its branches
which are many and many

and as they are not more specific
they loom, vague and impending.
bunched by breeze they move the hours
this way and that on a hot day.
encircled by a ring of streetlamps
this is a petrified monument.
starting here and ending there, it forms
an outline of the still and writhing.

then to see it next day,
its hands, large in the air,
applaud like loose thoughts
up and down the rigid landscape

june morning

june morning,
the tiles on the roof do not look like wounds.
no wind has yet blown a heap of words
behind all these dusty books.

so that's something already. at other times
telling ourselves things aren't like that anyway
we like the scenery: branches over roof,
a little bird or two on the branches.
on the tabletop the wind
blows up a bouquet of tiny alarms
scattering a glass and some empty smiles.

think sharp:
this scene is also very brittle,
copes with the problem of the accidental
to make it come more fully to life.
you look up from your thick black diary,
frowning, lines fragile as little bones

and it is you who structure this scenery

open road

breasting a tall crest of road
the sky looms. quick capricious illusion
pushes away two banks of rubber trees.
this looming sudden expanse
gathers itself like a sullen face
which over the plantation breaks,
unfurling tight-curled tips of the topmost leaves
with slip-drops of water falling, scattering
lean dogs with humpy shivers.

only the cyclist's heart
halts at the sightless road, wet with eyes.
wet with life, the plantation is its difference
from dry days, definable days
of heat and light lallang seeds.
while the grass usually sizzles with blade-rubs
it now bends green arches under an uncertain rainbow,

the road slices through two lives
which are the quick and, mainly, the quicker

evening

one thing to mark is lovely:
see the weight of sunset
perch convergent on the horizon
washed by tide culled from here,

seagulls rising
are erased by an arc of light
refracting direction of wings,
water out-folding
seals the earth beneath
and throbs over a mile of wind

tanah rata

I
look how this slope is paved
with yellow cosmos
nodding to butterflies

and alike to passers-by
like us returning from brinchang
followed by five o'clock
sun behind us,
look how the slope ends with grass
flanking blown cannas

to which we can add
the old woman weeding
nodding to flowers
gradually growing upwards
and ending where the slope begins

II
missing a step
the path crazily laid
with broken bricks
fallen casuarina leaves
and pockets of cold air

the child gathers himself up
to an unexpected smack,
his mother trundles on ahead
with a laden basket
lifts the latch of the gate
at the top of the path
turns back to the reluctant child
hauls him up with quick words

lays out vegetables
throws away wrapping paper
and lifting the child
kisses him, asks if he's hurt

from

COMMONPLACE

[1977]

for Keith

black & white

impact of collision, the long-legged road in convulsion.
2 school children, uniform-clad,
spread blue on the zebra-crossing. one, the other,
or both may not return from the brink.

a beautiful day. a new jaguar glides by.
all spectators shift focus: black & white to red,
draining into the spectrum of blood. 'must be at least
60 thousand'. 'who can afford such nonsense?'

black & white report. witnesses' testimonies.
respective heartaches. black & white dissolve
into grey. traditional chinese painters adduce 7 greys,
7 grey days a week. 7 dead zebras.

everything's coming up numbers

the death of the prime minister of china
left a wake of sorrow & a flock of numbers;
the death of the prime minister of malaysia
left a similar sorrow & a different set of numbers.
in market places, coffee shops,
the communal privacy of homes,
telephone & pencil were relaying numbers:
do we add 3 to his age?
put 6 at the end, or as the third digit?
do we follow the same for him as well?

the betting-booths displayed a list of numbers,
numbers already oversubscribed by collective certainty.
they were, therefore, not to be further abetted.
someone's death, it was felt, need not
incur one's corporate economic grief.

some bargirl's suicide. the old tree at the cemetery.
the wrecked mazda, the doubled-up honda,
their number-plates are shown in the papers clearly.
the little boy weaving between cars at the junction,
his mah-piew-poh may inform of remuneration.

everything's coming up numbers:
an old shoe with the manufacturer's code,
a child's first word at 2.30, wed., the 14th.,
a film star's number of stab wounds.
somewhere, someone, so many times, what;
what, where, somehow, who says so;
what figures, where, add which, whom,
you saw what time, how many, good or not.

some friends

one of my friends has green fingers,
she grows grasshoppers quicker than flowers.

another, always wanting to get me a better job,
peruses the classified ads. avidly for his next stop.

another, once a staunch undergrad socialist,
now scoffs at all stupid, rash idealists.

another, pitying the starving millions of the third world,
merely prattles & even this world becomes a blurr.

another, a devout practising vegetarian,
eats eggs with a heap of chopped onion.

another, who celebrates each & every religious festivity,
has given all gods a rest & taken up other civilities.

i have yet to meet them all at once
for fear of the confusion that will arise:
civil eggs with chopped idealists,
grasshopper jobs with fringe-benefit onions,
ex-green-fingered socialists, floral vegetarians.
(o gawd, another friend's injunction)

dog-eared

the only really shabby people i know of
are the rich, or those who imagine themselves so.
but the saints all had long hair,
tattered clothes (though a halo, if icon-ed)
& it's difficult to draw the line
between the contemporary shabby
& those so in the past.

if we believe in reincarnation,
the only really shabby people i know of
are saints of the past but, then,
they won't be rich, or imagine themselves so.
when they step off a plane (or mainly out of line)
they seem to take their poverty so becomingly.
this pleases no one,
irritates some who would tend to them
with words, glances or scissors.
(but step out like birds with appended plumage:
an entire ballroom is taken to reenact their passage).

the nouveau pauvre do not live in kennels,
they sit in penthouses & fume a little
if they have been misinterpreted.
sometimes, filling in forms & coming to 'occupation',
they do not write 'x's reincarnation'
but, frequently, (such-or-such).
it is not their business to be otherwise
or to understand why they are apostatized.

on reading a current bestseller

the naming of parts, never direct,
is nevertheless carefully alluded to. the lovers,
anatomised, have their parts, if not their roles,
served up to the eye: proxy voyeur.
a paragraph's a huff,
a page a pant.
(who was it ran a mile under 4 minutes?)

who is the grammarian?
the naming of the parts (of speech):
today's lesson, refer your eyes
to page 11, prepositions—
in, up, between,
up & down,
in & out.

today's follow-up, page 92, botany:
rose, core, flowering,
an arboretum where all blooms boom.

some flights have been stretched without much sweat.
much sweat, sometimes, without skin.

inventory

under repair:
slums, broken hearts,
robbers & robbers inc.,
plastic lips, doctored orders,
jack the ripped,
laws of gravity, potted rainbows,
roof tiles, latent heat,
cumulus clouds, inert gases,
cultural bilges & misc. eruptions.

undergoing change:
all those above.
solid geometry, liquid water,
potential energy, woeful weals,
bad manners, decent exposure,
culture vultures & dovetail joints,
elementary humanities,
second-degree burns & culpables,
malleables, shapeables, feasibles, plausibles,
probables, liables, viables, possibles,
finger-printed sandwiches.

notice on wall, flanked by a calendar
& a cockroach or two:

All repairs are subject to alteration without
prior notification. All clients are respectfully
requested to redeem their gift repair coupons by
the first of every month, instant, for purposes
of compilation. All repairs become null & void
within 3 minutes.

a circle

the kingfisher is said to fly so fast
it seems to be chasing after its own cries:
so the singer singing very loudly
appears to be chasing her own ears:
the deft tucks of the plastic surgeon
the former face is left in aberration:

somewhere
allthetime chasing:
the puppy after its tail,
the end after the beginning,
all sorts of ends for all sorts of means,
the crime to fit the punishment,
a Meaningful Arrangement of life
after a meaningful arrangement of fiction,
dry spasm for wet tears,
public grief for private traumas:
allthetime unending:

images unlimited:

dreams & reality pte. ltd.:

no directors, no operators:

all major & minor shareholders.

letter from a youth to his prospective employer

sir: i refer to my interview & your salary offer:
you said i would be given a commensurate salary:
commensurate with what? the depth of the filing
cabinet or the old bag sitting 3 desks & one right-
hand corner away? i am reasonably qualified:
quite handsome: my lack of experience compensated
by my prodigal intelligence: i shall not expect
to marry the typewriter: it's decision-making
i am after: that's what i am: a leader of tomorrow:
so why don't you make it today? my personality
is personable: & all opportunities being equal:
i am equal to any most opportune moment:
any most momentous opportunity: so take me
to your highest superior: & spare nothing:
at my earliest convenience: yours faithfully

north hill road, leeds

the few 11 pm lights are busy exchanging signals
with, above, the glinty stars:
little poke-holes on a large black tarpaulin
pegged down by nerveless wintry branches.
the frosty road raises itself up one hump
before dissolving in a flight of steps.

i'm already in my room
wallpapered with a few numbed thoughts;
all the books piled high on the shelf
make me think only of hot coffee.
looking out of the window, i see myself
walking up the road, down the steps:

this image i seem to see continually
as if it demands a profile
now that i'm no longer there.

new year '75, leeds

we wandered into a new year, as if by error.
at the chinese restaurant, my vietnamese friend & i,
the only asians, ordered 2 bowls of noodles.
the waiters served graces & teeming dishes
& the good laodiceans smiled warmly & scrutably.
our noodles finally arrived,
steaming under a turned-up nose.
vu's cossack-like cap still on his head,
my ears belonged once again to me in the warmth;
our cheer our tea, our leedsfraumilch 75,
kitchen-fresh vintage.

earlier, we had been to the plaza where x-rated films
are lined up each week, cheek by jowl. no psychological
reality, vu's comment. i forget if i had a rejoinder.
leaving the restaurant for our hotels, we passed
austicks, bookshop & frequent haven from the cold,
brotherton library, one side of woodhouse moor:
all somewhat remotely outlined in a thin swirling snow.
his hostel first, half a mile more for me:
everything behind were already soft-focal —
snow, steaming noodles, celluloid close-ups,
& night's myopia. next day, next year.

evening

bilabial at the edge of earth & water
stepping-stones like giant molars
grow old, grow dead.

under an aestival sun
daffodils have bloomed, dead
now, keening in a heap.

side-stepping these stones, people grow tired.
scattered images, mossed stones,
a fallen tree, annual rings felled:

sudden flare of an evening,
supposition of night blown by a slight breeze
right here, right now.

accelerando

so easily forgettable:
this baleful sky hangs like grey felt,
one rusty-toned star & defined silhouettes
of tall buildings nail in a large loom of despair.

slowly, with your umbrella,
you do not even talk of the weather.
rows of orange lamplight appear & dissolve,
move away to other eyes.
suddenly there is a screech of brakes,
or there isn't; a rude word in pedestrian collision.
swiftly, snowflakes are swirling down.
the sparkle of a little boy's eyes,
his brown mittens, sprinkled white,
are stretched out right into the sky.
the rusty-toned star drops out of sight.
the sky has swallowed the city
in one unforgettable gesture.

commonplace

daybreak, arms & legs.
breakfast. day lengthens: commonplace
situations & people. you say:
let's meet for lunch.

afternoon's 2nd movement, andante,
as if groaning a bit.
everything has happened before
but there is nothing to compare it
each time, with each time that it recurs;
& i should never whip the commonplace
for the meaning of its opposite,
especially at daybreak, with blue
shadows to protract into a shadowless noon.
2 o'clock: 2 stained blobs on a clear canvas,
3 o'clock: 3 fingers tapping a tattoo on the table
are 3 upwind gulls, sliding, side to side,
wings hung out still. now and then a small shrug,
only to gather lift for this weaving, unweaving,
white & grey shuffle, as playing at cards,
writing a letter.
4 o'clock: like yesterday's glance,
still holds true. this morning's streets
are already rattling cars & buses back
into younger & less immediate parts of the city.
commonplace evening, the place is the same.
when night comes, it will come in neonlights.
when night comes, will it come in darkness
or will it bring its own light to a well-scrubbed day?
will there be doubt that commonplace is?

& the tide

& the tide which is being urban-renewed
at bedok must go on its own tidy ways
without too much of a fuss,
coming in as riprap waves
met by the breakwaters
or going out sufficiently
for undisturbed analysis.
& the sum of their margin:
a littoral of slightly raised damp sand
& carefully arrayed litter.
out there where the waves curl,
the liquid is greenly uneven
in the sun's rays & the sky's
layers of noon darkness.
the renewal of a large imagination
may be rare, in a seascape.

there is no future in nostalgia

& certainly no nostalgia in the future of the past.
now, the corner cigarette-seller is gone, is perhaps dead.
no, definitely dead, he would not otherwise have gone.
he is replaced by a stamp-machine,
the old cook by a pressure-cooker,
the old trishaw-rider's stand by a fire hydrant,
the washer-woman by a spin-dryer

& it goes on
in various variations & permutations.
there is no future in nostalgia.

an afternoon nap

the ambitious mother across the road
is at it again. proclaiming her goodness
she beats the boy. shouting out his wrongs, with raps
she begins with his mediocre report-book grades.

she strikes chords for the afternoon piano lesson,
her voice stridently imitates 2nd. lang. tuition,
all the while circling the cowering boy
in a manner apt for the most strenuous p.e. ploy.

swift are all her contorted movements,
ape for every need; no soft gradient
of a consonant-vowel figure, she lumbers
& shrieks, a hit for every 2 notes missed.

his tears are dear. each monday,
wednesday, friday, miss low & madam lim
appear & take away $90 from the kitty
leaving him an adagio, clause analysis, little
pocket-money.

the embittered boy across the road
is at it again. proclaiming his bewilderment
he yells at her. shouting out her wrongs, with tears
he begins with her expensive taste for education.

the coffee house, cockpit hotel

not a daily occurrence:
a bride waiting, 7.30 pm, at a coffee house.
you, shifting eyes, forkfuls into mouth,
stop. stop & watch the bride,
2 bridesmaids & an elderly chaperon
at the little round table
having a respite before the dinner.
her eyes, downcast, become modest behaviour.

immediately one floor down
dragon room is taken for the reception.
relatives line up at the entrance,
the men clutching proffered tins of rothmans.

twice, a hand gently steals out & pats
any suspected flaw of coiffure into perfection.
most of the time, looking at her gloves,
her eyes are downcast, cast downwards
one floor immediately below.

at the end of an elastic hour
will she rise, raise her eyes,
descend one floor, ascend the low platform
elevating the tabled 10 courses,
smile gently at the groom, post-sharksfin
& pre-crispy chicken & mark out clearly
her domain, right here & right up there?

similes

like one of those refined persons
who go out to scrub for the rich
because they cannot abide contact with the poor:

the canker to the rose.
but sunflowers also burst from dung
& fingers of unfortunates wring out tunes,
tall buildings on reclaimed land.

like one of those refined persons
who go out to loll about with the lazy
because they cannot abide contact with the orderly:

the garden reverts to jungle,
the go-slows become die-offs.
the ants & bees
of society lose their ability
to tidy up in the wake of faded levis.

dawn

dawn in the quiet key of light
utters a whole paragraph of hues
in the early mutter of an aviary.

clear upward lift of night,
tensile & then quickly certain:
the lively key to morning
is mysteriously sharp, already laden
with the still, angular mirrors of noon.

the day obtains itself.
the evening obtains skies & dawn.

absolute

morning is already late
in rounding the corner of living,
windowpanes of tiny raindrops
cling uncertainly, left from night rain.

strange you are asleep,
often waking so early
to see the leaves weave
skeins of cool air between trees
at the corner of these buildings.
i think i'll get this in a picture,
hang it on a nail
& set the sky within its frame.

seeing,
i shall dispel dimness.
& sorry if i should awaken you;
i've gathered morning like a flower,
it doesn't smell for me.
(i can tell by the cheer in your eyes
you've never quite learnt to believe).
later, & still later of the morning,
morning it is,
& absolutely nothing is wrong.

another look

About suffering they were never wrong,
The Old Masters: how well they understood
Its human position.

Musée de Beaux Arts. W.H.Auden

how an adaptation
between canvas & the hand:
an old masterly breath
dispensed sectorial suffering.
here, where it all is going on
is not the locus; but further
up or down are the spatial reactions
for surprise or sadness.
never level, the locus, this suffering
has to be watched carefully.
the stabbed figure in convulsion
has a destiny to go into,
an explanation, an appraisal,
a catalogue-listing.

never level, this suffering, this locus:
what it is, the literal size
incorporates, & larger or smaller
than life, this resinous suffering,
less frenetic, keeps pace
with or without contemporaneous occurrence.

dracula

an eye-mixture of the modern & the past,
of the practical & the fancifully wild
(compounding channel 5 news with channel 8 fiction)
dracula's extravagant features melted
a pair of frightened but beautiful eyes,
her flushed & his comic face, so intent on badness,
i could not see him in the role of fiend.

a very wet &, as it seemed to me, transfigured stare,
an angry red puncture on her noughts & crosses throat.
on her throat there was that angry red tincture.
drac put his immortal hand to his stupid forehead,
& a cry in which joy & rehearsal seemed blended.
it was a recall associated with the giant bat
from hades, 2 man-eating spiders, 7
9-children eating frogs,
a sequel for which the world is tomorrow fully prepared.

things

chair
wall
window
desk
bed

chair makes us fat, upholstered in blubber.
long shot: wall. no one has ever succeeded

in being hung up like a portrait, truly dead.
medium shot: window. open it.
let the sun in, let suicide out.
before hitting the ground, frame it in slow motion.
reverse repeat, pan it back to window, its source.

to think up such imperfect realia
i'm at desk. it isn't true that one dreams in bed.

configuration

anything is better than stagnation,
the world seems big & kind enough to all;
a hongkong lady, daughter of a merchant
he had met in connection with the trading of jade.
the lady, very pretty,
began to show some curious traits,
quite alien to her usual sweet disposition,
to a charming & affectionate youth
unhappily injured, being shot at
in connection with the jade trade.
day & night the jade lady covered the youth
with prayers &, then silent, like an alert nurse
stayed in wait in case the child stirred.
his frame had fallen in,
his eyes were vacant.

(but the most loving heart within)
it seemed a childhood fall & a twisted spine
now righted, & her father's wealth, the lady
became celebrated. over his bowed shoulders
she laid her hands as if in benediction.
his wan looks like pale jade
which is life & death to her,
a physical puzzle to the doctor.
it is certainly delicate, said the man
who met her father in connection with jade.
up to now i've not been struck by its simplicity.

group dynamics 1

first, it was steamed eyes when the soup arrived.
eyes clear, glasses demisted, next the steamed fish stared.
was it for these we were there? dead pieties.

a speech after dinner, barer than the walls.
figures of speech of elation & ramification
didn't help. empty pieties.
dessert after dinner, longans & words.
a bit of leg-stretching, (not too much),
mustn't be seen with socks not pulled up.

elastic pieties, expandable by the hour,
relaxed conditionals:
if & then only if we weren't there,
if & then only if (unreal condition) the speech
weren't there, the speaker weren't there.
then, the soup wouldn't have,
the fish shouldn't.
& what's there left?
in absentia. in praesentia, weren't
                                      much

group dynamics II

reginald is 19, very smart & somewhat bored.
wingho is like reginald, without the honda sports.
benny is like wingho, both are wong.
may-lin comes from another school
& our pre.u's real strong, you know.

wingho calls may-lin sis & she giggles.
julie, also wong, thinks it's all so wrong
all this giggling, & i don't always want to go out.
she does if they are, (ring-ring) she's in, julie speaking.

let's chase them. reginald sped. stupid nut
may-lin said. stupid nut wingho said
to any driver reginald had overtaken.
to bedok julie said. go to bedok, you bodoh
wingho said. we'll send you a postcard, julie
indicated, forming an oblong with her fingers.
swiftly passed-by drivers registered no surprise.

next week let's go...
(a screech) simultaneously almost
the lampost quivered forward. thrown forward, julie
reached out as if to light it. reginald's face
wiped the sole of wingho's shoe. the windscreen wove
a spider's web. the mascot on may-lin's lap.
reginald's licence is suspended.
julie still sulks. may-lin doesn't worry,
she's going to university.
never mind what faculty
she puts the phone down on benny.
wingho is like reginald,
benny is like wingho.
they wait for the bus,
they wait for a taxi
to take susie & bee ngah
to the troika.
they wait for the call-up.

from
DOWN THE LINE
[1980]

in memory of) anthony (my brother

they are days

days are variable,
each day has what each day has.
that, which others haven't,
is best. its best is more
a constant. less best
is less everything lenitive.

they are variable,
each they has what each they hasn't.
this, which others have,
is better. but best is more
a concern. less best
is plus everything fugitive.

paper

paper explains many things.
its surface is skin
above-bone, grafted at eye-level.

egyptian papyrus,
chinese rice paper,
epidermis, stationers',
bonds, suicide notes,
minutes of meetings.
the latter 2 may be (maybe) writ in blood.

plastics takes many years to decompose.
paper doesn't, all the time endless succession:
heroes & villains who've rocked the boat
wade (only) downwards to find it,
not mud, is paper-given.
& freedom is paper. upwards, too,
every cloud has a papery lining.

shipwreck

shipwreck: i've written about it, & more, before.
with an island background, it had only been composed
upon in school. splendid shipwrecks, salted treasure
as easily scooped, a misgrounded fly from an ink-bottle.
the scope of fluent ignorance, my pen raced. at that age
i chased themes that were totally mine, weren't dreams.
it was a duty owed more myself than the pen.

about shipwrecks: were i in school now, i'm better able
to write on the velocity of wind, oscillations of tides,
the extent of salvage insurance companies need underwrite,
the structural implications on shocked timber.
can't i?

nowadays teems with more themes.

sheepwreck: (as i imagine) in animate collision,
each impact cushioned. do i say to you:
let us not pull wool over each other's eyes
(& other civilities)?
over to the ships' wrecked captains where it seemed
to have begun & then definitely ended,
to pirates marinated in seasonal winds,
to a harbour where eyes obtain like sardines:
a shipwreck is a tall shore of humanity.
with an island background, it had been composed
on sand, dry inland, crafted by hand.
it can be seen in the city, daily,
neatly.

medium

behind the fence-struggling morning-glory, you see 2 trees:
one is a fig tree, the other a (smaller) fig tree.
below one or the other sits a kampung chicken
equipped with a telephone, with or without an extension.
the kampung chicken's mouth is its lower effusion,
each time it squiggles, some shit (surely) drops out.
below the tree, this one or that, the telephone rings,
the kampung chicken squeals with delight over the
information.
listen, listen to how the leaves zing with activity.

the kampung chicken is itself a clearing house.
yesterday's lain egg is dead. it exults over such hatch
because, from that, it knows it existed yesterday,
that yesterday hadn't been a sloppy omelette.

behind the fence-hugging morning-glory, you see 2 trees:
one is a grapevine, the other a (quicker) grapevine.
look at the kampung chicken, it pimps for every ring
& prinks properly over every prime prize ping.

down the line

i.
the wind that weaves across buildings
carries the calculus the city is reckoned on.
call it what we will, it is liquid graphics,
neither statistics nor logistics can propel,
for its basis well under the skin has yet another
lined in rubrics & this, then, is palpable
& lends the eye whatever enchantment it wishes.
it will enchant with the cool young shadows
the sun, climbing vertically down windows,
leaves behind. it will enchant in its repose
by moving, shifting to the centre of its axiom,
in its layering of reality & in imparting
the sum of its being; every part, every space
larger & more real than the entirety.
if tomorrow someone sings a confessional
of some 'ism or other, the refrain sinks in
as only a totality & any event, being given,
predetermined, is at the onset already silent.
silently, the moon flanked by ribbed clouds
is jailed for influencing, or not, missiles
& this too holds no stored fear for tomorrow
it rains & the gurgling of drains, protomusic,
will soothe ancient nerves, iron out new alarms.

ii.
we say that a person who had stabbed himself
19 times & then thrown his own body over
the balcony is unbelievable reportage.
if you tell me times enough, tired, i will believe
or, at the least, agree. & if you tell me
times more, angered, i will throw
the narrated body back at you.

possible, too, i well might have believed.
so credulity is a bigger commodity than credibility
which is everybody's. the other, an exercise
of the mind, is yours if you can shape it.
breaking it, breakage is accidental
& never really necessary. a place-style
of impelling rhetorics, down the line,
foisting tautologies as ramifying definitions.

iii.

the tanned figures on the beach are not there
for further sun. noon, the heart's pulsation
without speech, is already late enough.
tenacious as weed, the crabs secrete bricks
& lay at the water's edge a library of margins.
page by page, it prefabricates the day's
ins & outs but, like pure callisthenics,
seems never quite enough. created thus to grow,
the calculus will help or quell us.
i thought the ground had foretold all.

a habit by which the world moves, people will not
look at the centre of things. the custodian must
find some flaw about his own belief to show up
those, accusing him, as punitive. wrong,
that in his pursuit, he does them good
purely by chance. such coincidence is a gift
&, in these days of libs, isn't it lib & let lib?
when the verb fails, everything ancillary
has only its chronicle of current antiquity.

grass replaces grass, fast. down the line,
dry, roots are cast. garden-to-garden green grass
calls to the eye an explication of beauty
& beauty, in the colouring heart of the beholder,
is not what suffices or does not. that it does not
comes last.

iv.

what everyone will tell you is what everyone
wants to hear, has been told. the clouds
have no radio & cannot relay silver linings,
glosses, appendices. we hear, what told,
wheels of woe, a battery of ear-assault
pooling in the lymph. the years,
if they have brought us no wisdom, would have
exploded the myth our images hold, rearranged
the calefaction of the thermometer
we regulate by.

night scene I

the warmth had left the west. timid
the stars appeared. preparedly, in the distance
a finger of light waved across the sky.
others too appeared &, higher or lower,
all impressed their lines on the blackboard sky.
quickly they are disambiguated,
the solitary finger is left
to write the margin of the next sunrise.

night scene II

the roofs drank in all the stars.
from the high evacuated space of sky,
visual acuity: tiny ambient arrows,
eyes opening like daisies
tomorrow. on the promenade,
soggy stars. one day later
the place is young again,
stars hooking up the roofs
in the high evacuated space of sky.

would it have been

would it have been different if it were not an apple
but a bomb which bit the world into being

&, whatever the conditionals, would it be different
after the bite, the lingua franca of the world
were sign language, metalanguage, antilanguage,
argot, braille, ipso facto esperanto,

houses were nests & people prefabricated
soyabean sculptures,

sunlight falling on a field burnt grass
into terminal rainbows,

cities held to ransom by their own devils
or collective dream sequences

: would it be very different if all these things
have had being been untrue?

a lesson on the definite article

a crowded restaurant, open eavesdropping
graded into one another's ears. sharing table:
a bearded man, a girl with bank-teller's eyes;
they arrived after me, & an umbrella & 2 coats
which were there when i was.

i really love chinese food, you people can cook
beautifully. the bearded man had also a large appetite.
i can't cook, & her non-sequitur
'the poor chinese are like the 2nd class jews'
provoked these possibilities:
poor chinese are like 2nd class jews,
poor chinese are like the 2nd class jews,
the poor chinese are like 2nd class jews.

the she was, by the way, the chinese
& her the accent, showing she had arrived,
gone the places, reached the it,
made the it, confirmed she was the.

the grammar of a dinner

let's have chicken for dinner.

somewhere else, someone else utters:
let's have john for dinner.
we are alarmed by the latter
but a dinner, too, has its own grammar
& we are assured by grammarians
both utterances are in order.

john, + animate, + human,
couldn't be passed off as repast.
chicken is + animate, - human,
& can end up in any oven.
if we combine the items of grammar
the way things in cooking are,
we would then have:
let's have chicken for john for dinner,
let's have chicken for dinner for john,
let's have for john chicken for dinner,
let's have for dinner for john chicken;
but probably not:
let's have john for chicken for dinner,
let's have for dinner john for chicken.

john is a noun holding knife & fork.
chicken collocates with the verb eat.
grammarians favour such words
as delicious & john eats happily,
but in a gastronomic dinner
taxonomic john isn't to eat deliciously.

event

a little combed & frilled girl, smile older,
at her wedding, the aunt's. combed & frail,
smile smaller, the bride's teeth stuck to her gums.
the occasion gave it beauty.

combed & frilled, the bouquet (waved about
like a microphone) picked up congratulations.
hands down, on the table 2 gloved mice.
(& another piece of peking duck for you?)

event.
eventually, the bride will be
at the little girl's wedding.
& peking ducks will get eaten
by other 2 gloved mice
in careful pieces.

roll call

i can understand animals in a zoo:
aren't they for our enjoyment?
i can understand their entertainment:
if they turn a few tricks for us
do we not give them some peanuts?
i cannot understand the zoo in me:
why i eat peanuts, am sometimes absurd.
i understand why i cannot be a zoo:
first of all, i wear glasses.
next, i don't particularly like mud,
turd & other such esoterica.
&, finally, i'm not very sure
of the heuristics of such phrases:
'social interaction' & 'behavioural objectives',
which i hear often
& which seem applicable to all animals.
because i can't understand them
i want to object to the phases
of (be)having to interact with them.
believing they must do their thing(s),
there'll always be a zoo. i shall go on
giving them peanuts & eat some myself
(not necessarily simultaneously)
)& would you like some as well?(

samson & delilah

they gave her a pair of scissors to cut his hair.
she didn't & they made love, there on the floor.
the bedridden grandmother wondered why the young,
always so noisy, were then fighting on the floor.
she must ask that boy never to come again.

the parents, on the rise, are breeders of girl guides,
they grow more grave as they grow more serious.
the youngsters, she is theirs, rising, are gone.
but she, who is theirs, will ask him to come again, soon.

worse & worse,
his hair not shorn. the other parents were afraid
their district was being given a bad image.
bad image: that noisy boy, on the floor,
hair shorn, listening to the rolling stones.
they didn't need give her scissors anymore.
she hadn't, & they made love, there on the floor.
the bedridden grandmother was dead,
dead to the noisy fight. hair shorn, gone
was the need to keep the long-standing irritation
over all other ordinary human volition.

rsvp regrets only

the ability to read road maps
or do sums, for example, can be described
in terms of an invitation.
one can always ask a further question
about any invitation: what's the good
of learning placenames, peoplenames, & how many
litres are there to the gallon?
unasked, regrets only.

the trouble, though, is that of deciding
what sort of thing is necessary to make
an invitee's autonomy. is it logically
necessary to be unable to prattle,
flip a drink neatly down, or what?
the card is invitational &, therefore, purportedly
carries a value, judgement it does not.
not that it means
regrets are what are being invited.
it is, after all, a filler problem.
the ability to read a number,
use a dialling finger, for example, can be
circumscribed in terms of a contingency.

in memory of) anthony

your coffin had no nails.
years i have lived with this nailed feeling,
every moment forgotten. & other moments,
larger remembrances, are also of you.
when all is said & not forgotten,
may it be known to me
& leave behind, not necessarily
even a need to understand
what you all along would know,
this long, long trail of quick, sharp sorrow.

for...

'The world is too much with us; late and soon,'
$$\text{Wordsworth}$$

never late. the current world is too soon.
my parents: one retired, one a housewife,
protected now as they have protected. all along
they have, after all, some of us,
our antiquated smallpoxes. our current problems
they cannot understand & why need they?

right now, i wish for them
what i think i can do, but don't
& they, i don't know if i'm right,
won't accept because they have
given & we, having taken,
now wanting to give, find it all given.
my parents, i'll never give you roses,
jade, accolades (or other such nonsense).
when it clarifies, i'll offer whatever
& i know it will be only a token
of what you, all along, have given.

until

until anthony passed away
i never saw cheeriest optimism
a person leaving hospital,
family carrying bags & he himself.

words

words have sometimes a way of stilling themselves
& then, no, we have a way of stilling words
in a way to still ourselves:
a choice of being still
& quiet to be still.

words need people to fill their blanks,
quick eye-flicks across the page:
a page of contained dimensions
housing a pharynx
that, from edge to edge,
is still,
still as a minute glottal sphinx.

postlude

the morning when requiem for her husband,
newly dead, was said, the evening saw
her new bridal gown brushing up the aisle.

little was said. the few guests at the reception
heard the bride, laughing, would keep her bouquet.
she wouldn't throw it, like defence, at their faces.
her & his children were eating cake.

mime

because the learner sat down
& regurgitated like an open book
para qua para he was taken as a clown.
he wasn't praised for his neat memory.

when the clown stood up
& gurgled like an open sewer
line by line he was taken as funny.
he was praised for his neat mimicry.

because mime is excruciation
ransacking each gesture is eristic.
because excruciation is excruciating
masks that appear in real situations
are worse, & what comparison is possible
when every mask wears a face?
faces mime faces mime faces.

late-night bonus

several teenagers, gathered together
for some organized disorder, have pushed over
a bin & were dancing round our (un)broken bottles.
jostling & shouting, it was quickly over.

of all a sudden i heard midnight laughter,
the 3-houred teenagers back with bicycles.
then jangling bells were quickly gone with the riders.
i remained awake & by linking the sense of speed
with darkness, the sense of place seemed destroyed.
the physical world will return tomorrow
but a moment's loss will not be gone.
& public durances & private aftermaths
every street has known.

a solid laughter theirs, however.

traffic

asked the way to park street
the old man drew himself up,
his shell of woollens seemed unburdened
&, fully intent to edify,
at great pains & greater length...

like any big city, this city
offers her people a variety of ways
in which moments of unhurry
may be used. the old man knew
roads never look like themselves,
edging sideways from the curb,
pushing over zebra zips. nevertheless...

& done. rounding a corner a little quicker
than cars, one's eyes read the restaurant's menu
for 'long soup' & 'short soup'.
feet, hesitating speculatively,
are like the feet on the cinema poster,
'porcelain anniversary', a french
concoction of limbs. simulated coitus,
long soup, streaking cars
blue to the gills, brick-clogged pores:
a connection of many things
that cannot undergo any physical editing.

most of october

the landscape is too empty. it threatens to dissolve
& include me in it. it threatens in a series of vast sizes
&, above all, in its indifference. the huge vastness
is always enlarged by some motion: a bird in flight,
a dazzlingly white sail slicing like a slow penknife.

seen through a huddle of wind-torn bushes at cliff edge,
the extravagant surf below pounds a silence to completion.
i cannot hear anymore the amplitude of wing,
wind & other sea-wounds.

the first thing to do is to drop a stone down the cliff
without dropping myself. i don't quite fit into this
landscape & there aren't even trees to give
a similar vertical accent. it needs entire absorption
& i'm not sure i want to throw away my shoes
as a start. i look at the sudden influx of sails
& it's almost like painting by numbers.
but before each square is begun
the others are already marvellously completed.

sights

the sights are like every city's offerings.
the difference is that, here, it is possible
to combine country & sea, a lovely
bilocation for the economy tourist.

on the hydrofoil, you know land
isn't distant. every cliff has a pair of hands:
the stone, the flower, nothing undefined
in the profile. birds cry across the bridge.
the evening sun walks up the cove
& drops smartly into slopping eyes.
you can hear your own fascination.

you turn a corner to a choked car's strangulation
&, from somewhere, a carried peal of bells.
sunsteeped stained-glass, the old enchantment
doesn't hold. at the turnstile, you may remember
something small: a packet of handmade paper
in a shop, a pinecone among grass,
how the coin spun & spun in the booth.

an accumulated store of sights,
the minuscule compress of days, the lovely passage
of quiet water, upward wind.

at balmain

quota of dogshit here & there
& the noon absence of dogs.
an old couple sunning
in an ornate wrought-iron porch
(paint peeling like leathery skin)
watched us assemble camera & tripod
with curiosity growing. the old woman,
hard of hearing, rapped out at the man,
her eyes never once moving from us:
what are they doing?
are they television?
& then to us:
gosh, aren't you started?
gosh, now i know who you are,
you can film the whole street for all i care.

i don't remember what the film was about,
every frame, anyway, out of focus. but etched clearly
in memory, the old woman's curlers
danced the way to the wharf
& became giant crests of waves.
the old man's toothlessness
the open space of the nearby park,
& a sibilant breeze
rapidized from balmain's throat.

i think (a book of changes)

when we came, it was all for grabs;
you might say the motivation was a quick dollar.
then those men came & demanded monthly payments
for 'your protected interest'. it makes life hard,
harder when you think of the pilferers.
a shirt here, a length of material there —
all gone as if into thin air.
but all this has gone on since those television
emperors' tombs & so the protection & the pilferage
isn't the story of this market.
the story is the story of change.

some people give you $5 & ask for change
from 50. this month, french knit is popular.
made in hongkong, the label's changed to u s a.
you don't wrap things up in straits times
or nanyang siang pau anymore, brown paper
isn't even good enough. change to plastic bags,
said one customer, with a pattern of red flowers
for luck. we've changed our name 3 times.
first, 'sincere shirts' was considered common.
everyone's sincere about business, so why be blatant?
next, we called it 'lucky store'. one week later,
my wife found another such store in the next section.
the owner had died. so when we were rightfully
the only lucky, we didn't want to be.
now we call it as it is: 'ah beng fabrics'.
next year we go over to that tall block,
7th floor. we shall call it 'number one stop'.
got to time in with the changes.
what?
what do i think of it?

2 mothers in a h d b playground

ah beng is so smart,
already he can watch tv & know the whole story.
your kim cheong is also quite smart,
what boy is he in the exam?
this playground is not too bad, but i'm always
so worried, car here, car there.

    at exam time, it's worse.

because you know why?

    kim cheong eats so little.

give him some complan. my ah beng was like that,
now he's different. if you give him anything
he's sure to finish it all up.

    sure, sure. cheong's father buys him
    vitamins but he keeps it inside his mouth
    & later gives it to the cat.
    i scold like mad but what for?
    if i don't see it, how can i scold?

on saturday, tv showed a new type,
special for children. why don't you call
his father buy some? maybe they are better.

    money's no problem. it's not that
    we want to save. if we buy it
    & he doesn't eat it, throwing money
    into the jamban is the same.
    ah beng's father spends so much,
    takes out the mosaic floor & wants
    to make terazzo or what.

we also got new furniture, bought from diethelm.
the sofa is so soft. i dare not sit. they all
sit like don't want to get up. so expensive.
nearly two thousand dollars, sure must be good.

    that you can't say. my toa-soh
    bought an expensive sewing machine,
    after 6 months, it is already spoilt.
    she took it back but...beng,
    come here, come, don't play the fool.
    your tuition teacher is coming.
    wah! kim cheong, now you're quite big.

come, cheong, quick go home & bathe.
ah pah wants to take you chya-hong in new motor-car.

fiscal ear

mr song, on the telephone, lets known
he's the head of the organizing committee.
he wonders why the caller wants to be so stingy.
does he not know how to do things in style?
mr song, on the telephone, will have none of that,
nor unnecessary worries: don't worry,
what you want to be so stingy for?
make sure there's plenty of v s o p.
mr song, on the telephone, orders smoked duck,
braised scallop with kai lan & many others
without need to consider any fiscal bother.
who wants to eat sweet & sour pork these days?
you want to eat sweet & sour pork?
& 4 taiwanese singers too, 3 are neither
here nor there.

mr song, later at home, wonders who has given them
those presents strewn on the table: who gave us
all these presents? mr song, at home, shouts
about the purchases his wife got from the emporium:
you think i print money? he wonders if his wife
thinks he prints money & whether she thinks
they're holland rd millionaires. i don't care
if it's annie's birthday. food is food.
why 3 tins of abalone? dried scallop!
you take them back & get a refund.
mr song, at home, wants his wife
return some abalone, scallop
&, while he's going at it,
& while she's about it,
tins of longan, a large packet of mushrooms,
& these as well, this, that also lah
(& blah).

from
MAN SNAKE APPLE
[1986]

for Miyuki Nagaoka

tropical paradise

the feel of things. textures. the elastic skin,
gently pliant to the touch. the cold metallic shock
of water in a shaded pool, galvanizing all the pores;

paradise:

staminate & pistillate, they all dance to the thrall of
primeval rhythms. things, things growing so fast; feel the
heat of their regeneration. the friction of leaf against leaf,
bud & bee, pod to pod. among the green mysteries of
certainty, they consume the decay of aged life:

paradise:

at sunrise, a stone falling endlessly
& in it the silence of before & after.
in the silence of before & after, a new stone
falls endlessly &, before it is done,

a head falling.
o lord, it is to you it falls.

jungle, a tall tree falling eternally.
& in it the rapidizing of leaves, stirred birds.
in the timelessness before & after, a new tree
falls within the fallen. being done,

a limb falling.
o lord, it is to you it dies.

stained glass

stained glass
was awesome silence,
was such quiet it indicated paraphrases everywhere.
the branches outside were your fingers
held in benediction.

god was such stillness,
his stained-glass figures stretched
neither forward nor backward in himself.

& at this ruby-amber corner
i could only gaze & piece together
whatever i had want of. i was free
because i was free from myself;
a mere witness in whom arose a great need,
urging like silent desperation, prayer,
to be included. i could be a mote, kill glass,
a sunsteeped blob of blood. a nothingness.

god, such stillness was.
your fingers were there.
what do you hold up to bless?

still-life 1

if she sits out in the garden, she's a pile of leaves
with a face. sunk in an armchair, it has an extra pair
of arms, gaunt. day in, day out, she's an arrangement
with different settings. a crab near the kitchen table,
a photograph of a head above a brown dress.

she will not move.

her hands & feet twist like vine, against her heart,
against its wish to be drawn apart.
why did you come into this world?
to pay back all my debts.

turning around in quietness, she lets a rasp
slip across the back of her paper hand.
new day, old familiar ache. it never reneges
into oblivion; always there, its intensity
spans a dull throb to the stab that amazes the flesh.

brooding silence filled with enigma & wonder;
nothing to threaten her now, this pile of leaves.
nothing to threaten now,
nothing to threaten now.

still-life IV

the friends' conversation still ranges
across the past as it spreads still
around the table. they ask questions,
not probing into one another's lives.
they would not care to admit what they cannot.
the children are held in the present,
staring over plates & cups. they have no demands
to make of anyone. they have nothing to remember
or to forget. they know exactly what is, isn't,
going to happen next. they cup their faces,
lovely, without a cause to decorate.

still-life v

where does rigour end & rigor mortis begin?
so slender is the distinction, & practice
ensures the perfection of numbing the sensibilities.

where does this counter end & the library begin?
faces looking out of spines to say: look,
this is me & me only. you are my sensibilities
& i wear your heart, your eyes, in my footnotes.

where does this park end & begin again?
do not be misled by the park. it begins & ends
every morning; its attendants arriving,
its lovers departing.
where does this pond end & its bank begin?
it begins in a moist susurrus of ripples
& doesn't ever end, even at the edge
of its beginning where wild watercress grows.
nothing is happening,
a non-event at no time recorded for posterity.
yet, there's a still pond wants to be fed,
a pond wherever it outlines.
& it doesn't especially want anything to happen
except it's a sunny day
with watercress soughing at its side.

still-life VI

something wonderfully familiar about the old lady
selling her jade bracelet; the old goldsmith
in the courtyard dallying with the pretty serving maid.
the old sage, intent upon his pagan loves,
his adoration of god, nevertheless saw every moment
of these sad allegories of human folly:
the gambler's ruin, the libertine's.
how this tripling composite picture would be swept aside.
& how out of this meaninglessness would come order.
orderlies to clean the courtyard,
polish the bracelet, spin loves & bring again
something wonderfully familiar: the old lady
selling her jade bracelet, the old gentleman
dallying with the old lady, the serving maid
with her bracelet & her sage.

man snake apple

ages the apple slept on the tree
dreaming of stars & storing the distillation
of a thousand storms, outlasted cheiroterous ravages
& survived more golden-red if the moons also blessed.
the snake jounced up & down the tree,
investigated the apple from all round angles,
a circumoral need. but it had no need to feed.
the apple had no meaning. man was trying out
& being tried out by his circumstance.
apple snake man were one, two, three.
the snake could rise & walk over man, the apple
of the circumambient eye. man could walk
slither-poised, hang on branches like a growth.

this was day one,
the first day from anytime.

& all days were easy. all ways led to the way
of the lie. it was the dry season, it was the monsoon,
& what should the land produce? young, the lie of the land
produced prodigiously, floriferously;
dazzling, giddying itself. man looked at everything
with the calm of unknowing eyes & did not want.
he remained empty till he did; the lie outright.
the apple lay absolute on the tree, the snake near.
man was somewhere between apple & snake.
he could no longer fly; his wings were lain still

this day,
day two

of whatever calender wasn't.
butterflies flew with the snake that changed

more swiftly than a spectrum of rainbows on short-loan
& the apple effloresced into protoneons; red, gold,
purple, a runnel of liquids & fugitives, visions.
man looked & felt the first flash of the pain of beauty.
the apple stirred in his heart, its stalk a tuning fork
regulating the earth, orchestrating symphonies of mountains,
suzerain dragons that immolated in hauteur.
the sun shone relentlessly white, clarifying the land
like fool's gold. & man performed marvellous feats.
trees grew from his fingers, his ears cornucopias.
but the lie was lain & the splendour could only go on
increasing, increasing, increasing with compound vigour.

(come off it.) onto day three, still increasing.
the fantasy was necessary feed for its own fodder.
there was still no other need
man snake apple
on day four, a day of lull,
a day of unearned blessedness;
the long rays of the sun
dripping like arrows of candlewax,
as small mercies, small-time alarms.

they disappeared on day five
because day five was day five
& all prior pluses & minuses
were not cued this day,
not gathered, not resown, not wanted.

& without the fore-days' diurnal dovetailings,
the day gathered itself as a flower before nightfall,
sufficient for its own context of being, untroubled
by vanity, anxiety or effort, or even happiness.

day six began with a short lineal history
of ancestral promptings & urgings,

a surfeit of wide-awake dreams, of ersatz violence.
it was a weight-lifter who couldn't get the weight up.
from morning to noon, from noon to dusk,
storing upon itself, conserving to have itself reborn.
an umbilication of comatose inertia. the finagling snake
quiet as coiled repose. the voluptuous apple slept on,
heavy as a stone, a minuscule pumpkin.
& ruminative man, poised as his own shily shadow;
an indefinable, incalculable weight on his shoulders.
the apple in his head slow-rattling, a feral football;
the snake in his heart undulating in lazy loops.

day six died.
the world grew young & day seven happened;
a minimum of event, fanfare, cheer-leading.
sun, moon, stars were freshly reordered.
man snake apple multiplied; in endless succession,
the progeny. men killed snakes, ate apples.
apples, detached from trees, dropped on men
& germinated ideas, created patents,
became the targets of crossbows.
snakes bit into serum & have carried it ever since;
popped out of watering holes, appeared in circuses,
slid over tarmac lanes, were run over by cars.

man snake apple were no longer one, two, three.
a fused combination, the progeny in infinite permutations.
mensnakesapples built cities, flew as they once did,
fought wars, archiving them as later documentaries,
invented organized leisure, civilized swindle,
top-ten everything, mass trances, pop-whatever.

it was forever & forever & forever

& a day,
today. it begins again today.

your goodness

for Keith

your goodness, i sometimes light
my anger with, is what you have. no one
can burn it away; it is not for my discussion.
i know, near you, i myself feel good.
& this is enough for me, my friend.

this is a life-time friendship; the poem
is short, inadequate &, except for a word,
totally redundant.

dialogue

unused to central london late on a sunday,
how brightly lit the shopfronts are
& how entirely dark the office windows above.
the place looks dead & alive at the same time.

from here to sloane gardens: out of the station,
i'm not sure whether to turn left or right
& this must be the many of many times.
but i'm here. you are at the door
&, walking up the steps, i have nothing to say.

if i tell you quickly: & told quickly,
it will be a truest instance. other times,
other such retellings are tautologies,
self-mimes of that better.
i do not admire the plant on the sill, shrivelling.
i do not thank you for dinner: it is the best.

i talk to you as you talk to me.
tomorrow morning now it is,
i leave & walk out of whatever station.
i walk further because it is not whatever time
& the cleaner might not have done the room.
i look at the shops & they are all the same.
i look at people & they all do not look like you.
i'm back; the cheeriest is the pot of daisies
bought whatever days back. i sit on whatever bed.
the room is all disappearing.
i walk out & look at more shops. they are all
very interesting; i don't know what of.
& you are at the door. walking up the stairs,
do you have anything to say to me?

in the quiet of the night

in the quiet of the night
when alert ears pulse sound
i can hear again the words,
the poet i was earlier reading:
he is one person i understand fully.
i understand he is a poet
& i understand his poetry.
i even understand my own knowledge
of this privacy which is public literary study.

the words will move on more swiftly
than tomorrow will be now. & i will
know, in reading again,
i do not know him
or any other, or myself, or that any poetry
is the public transaction that it must be.
& it must be private ultimately.

when last seen

three things he said & her reply
rang with domestic despair.
there he lurked, practising his cruelty.
too suddenly her sadness overwhelmed
&, behind familiar things, a new keen
hate & that, subsiding, erased
her sadness. her regret & shame
seemed to flow through her fingers;
the prepared vegetables definitely tasted
too oily; her snakes-&-ladders emotions
the chequered dishcloth. three times the drain gurgled
& her request rang with clarity.
there he lurked, practising his plumbing.
the snakes & ladders slithered down,
carrot ends & chillie seeds & onion roots.
as he got up she threw the dishcloth,
his face the draughtsboard. she saw distinctly
a softening of his features &, stepping forward,
shed all her tears into the sink.

dinosaurs

After visiting the 1964 New Generations show of paintings and sculptures at Whitechapel, Keith Vaughan wrote:

> After all one's thought and search and effort to make some sort of image which would embody the life of our time, it turns out that all that was really significant were toffee wrappers, licquorice allsorts and ton-up bikes...
> I understand how the stranded dinosaurs felt when the hard terrain, which for centuries had demanded from them greater weight and effort, suddenly started to get swampy beneath their feet. Over-armoured and slow-witted, they could only subside in frightened bewilderment.

Keith Vaughan, *Journal and Drawing*, 1966

the dinosaurs were reactionary;
had no other bulk acceptance
to push back the pace. often inconvenient
& mismanaged, still the world
to them was accustomed kindness;
they basked in the sun which was round & real,
not a suspended soft sculpture, a cybernetic disc.
when the sun changed conceptually
& one more light was piled upon the vatic mind,
the quiet weight fermented the images that fed the eye.
they lumbered as they walked, sidled sideways
from toffee wrappers & licquorice allsorts.
the oblique approach was the safest; the truth a gait.
within the cage of modernities, the dinosaurs prowled,
looked for exits: expressed themselves somehow,
sometimes eloquently, crossing the swampy gap
without the help of souped-up bikes.
but no dinosaur could entirely submerge
without resurfacing in a museum,
a new-generation contemporaneity,
as no meaning could go away
without returning upon itself.

street scene 1

shaking the match long after it was dead,
as if it were a pioneering gesture for fire,
the man asked of me:
do you know the hours for reduced rates?
i had no such vital knowledge, being a visitor.
putting the match back into the box,
as if it were to be a sealed ecological artefact:
you don't know then, he said with certainty
of my ignorance. i knew i had to check & know
this bit of information, suddenly very necessary.

i did not. but, before i didn't, i watched him,
wearing his woe with a proprietorial air,
walk to someone else. perhaps he asked it again.

of such questioners there are two:
one who goes truly hoping to find answers
& one who secretly hopes he won't.
i think he didn't want to ask anything
except: why am i so lonely & have to stop you?
i felt the same then. as he walked on,
he seemed to grow larger & larger,
ignoring the laws of perspective.

street scene II

there can never be too many people in the street.
immediate evening, the afterimage is a bitter glow
of neon moons creating their own sky.

the street is neither too long nor too short
for the night, too, is neither.

& by losing oneself, the solipsist's nightmare
in which everything exists but oneself:
a big foeval eye.

foursome

as we were talking, she thrust her head,
regular as a metronome, & rapped orders at him
& the dog. a finger-shaking woman, full of injunction
for man & beast. whenever she called out in her pained
pinched voice, i would watch her, he me, & the dog him.

with the first peal of thunder, the dog raced a circle.
her finger shaking became critical. he turned to lower
a bamboo blind; was shut off. i could see the dog
full of indignation against the thunder & lightning
she was the goddess of. & he, long ago, must have stolen
the first embers to flame his household with little crises,
necessary to outlast all the next days.

exchanges

because he was so old & inexpensively untidy,
the alliteration of the cash register & the fingerer's
ice-cube laughter. she thought the cans of dogfood
were for himself, a damn silly old sod.

she was so painted & bouffant, & her escutcheon
of a skirt wouldn't have hidden a can of worms;
he thought her a whore. up there, dogs, catfood.

through all the month of days, the silent exchanges
raced with the clarity of cellophane over fresh-cut ham.
when he bought watercress, he was a drowning man,
an old dog with a granite collar, a seaweed stew.
her heavy breasts over the keys; no wonder cows play
the yamaha with their udders. what's this chalky liquid
in the plastic bottle? have you given it your all?

to celebrate the cerebral prior to physical potentials:
here's a pot of green syphilitic-looking ceterah,
cakes like trod-on dung, pneumatic mangoes, choices galore.

alternation

Then, at college, in a single day I decided to change my
handwriting...which meant, I realized later, a change in the making
of words which even then were all of me I cared to have
admired...I sat down with the greatest deliberation and thought
how I would make each letter of the alphabet from that moment
on...
Well, that change of script was a response to my family situation
and in particular to my parents. I fled an emotional problem and
hid myself behind a wall of arbitrary formality.

    William Gass, *Writers At Work, The Paris Review Interviews*

s simple act orthographed with complexity
deliberating shaped lines on paper.
what is it for but oneself, out of joint?

look at the columns of linears deployed
on the surface: should they make cosmetic sense,
no ontogenic sense is gained. the paper cuts something
between them and their beginnings. more powerful,
more sustaining than real-life familiarities;
to appear on one's own screen would vindicate

a whole existence.
                        they exist for the nonce,
these emergent alpha-beta angels & float
in any meaning willed to them. pulsed to a tether,
will you let them

be? or you free?

immediate capsule history; a recognition moves
in memory. they have all been here before.
the brilliant hand radiating a crisp clutch of letters,
too, never forgets where it's been & it's been
over these stretches many many times.
today, there can be ten reasons for the changes,
tomorrow might see another ten new ones.
there isn't a single, disappointing, unchanging answer.

eyes

I know thy works, that thou art neither cold nor hot:
I would thou wert cold or hot.
Revelation 3:15

i spoke the only words for the entire duration:
thank you, eyes. something troubled,
the eyes were very sad.

either hot or cold, the eyes were very sad.
a rule of eyes: be careful in the search
of adventure, it's very easy to find.

the eyes were sitting there, tidy mental bundles.
the clever eyes, which steal people for their existence,
line a face never creased. never very tidy.

never hot or cold.

nightjar

here, in the night, trees sink deeply downward.
the sound of moonlight walking on black grass
magnifies the clear hard calls of a nightjar,
its soliloquy of ordered savagery, little intervals.
time, clinging on the wrist, ticks it by
but eyes, glued to the dark pages of night,
could not scan the source on the branch.

its insistent calls jab & jab so many times
to a silent ictus, so many times, ringing off the branch
in tiny sharp *tuks,* each lifting from the last

through the night, while the shadows of the trees
go past the edge of sleep & i sit awake,
if it's footfalls across the road, they should be
far away, sounding on the trees, an euphony
lodged on high, the starlit side of heaven.

paraphrase

when one wonders how to begin to talk
about something, the word swallows the world.
the word comes close to carrying its own ontology,
its own reward for being:
                              all the way to hākone
words were hung on every tree. the most striking,
startlingly orange, tuned by the breeze.
words, maple leaves. words were brown moss,
mellow sunlight with soft hair.

words were on the lake; sea-mews spanning circles,
white on white foam of the boat's wake. a translucent mist
held the banks in check. then, a sudden reined splash
of muted colour, a shape proffered itself. the image beckoned
the eye, a word whispered itself: it's a blue moored boat,
a clump of willows. words were a crocodile of schoolboys
jostling & laughing on the deck.

the lake was a sheet of glass; everything a smaller mirror
beneath. on the surface, a catamaran floated us,
words, all the way to hākone, words were.

a good poem

They know how to enjoy themselves without ceasing to be good boys and girls.
                                        Miyuki Nagaoka

so do we.
too, we are good. you, good boys & girls,
how in enjoying yourselves are you
in such completion, mutual absorption.

& how the marvellous colours flow:
your clothes, her scarf, his redolent words.
you are the regenerative peacocks of this world.
today, i am a sparrow pecking at the earth,
the rainbow, the cloud storing a complete typhoon.

excuse us, we also want to go up.
from the huge glass window, the rail tracks
spread out like the ribs of a fan. no,
i don't want a coffee, you are taking me
to mimiu for udon suki. let's to down.
the lift is full of good boys & girls.

too.

the shisen-do

A ZEN GARDEN IN KYOTO

you can almost hear the sap raise newer leaves.
past the simple rustic outside-gate,
a slightly ascending passage with stepping-stones
leads to the inside-, the garden front.
the interior garden reveals shaped azalea bushes,
sand combed into a pattern, a spent wisteria,
little white daisies. a low waterfall,
the clacking of the sōzu. not too many flowers,
not too many lives.

the woman bending over some plants
thought they were a kind of chrysanthemum,
her words never once staying her tending hands.

no photographer to record the scene, to fail.

a bowl of green tea, a biscuit on a paper square.

always the same tableau, intrinsically still,
the kindling of every sentience.
it is always the same & one can see
it had always been, will be.

12-times table

a scenic depiction is always inexorable
being exclusive right down to its very agencies:
grass, water, sky, hills. the two worlds,
that depicting & that transmogrifying beyond,
beyond grass, water, sky, hills; the two worlds
can come to no direct contact. yet without such contact
no evocation of a transfer is possible:
                        an arm for a branch,
                        a ear for a sliver of bank,
                        an eye for a pod,
                        a heart for age-rings.

it was at gifu. it was at osaka.
it was blue-&-white ceramics at gifu;
it was amethyst ceramics at osaka.
camellias, egg-plants, pines: designs of the fingers.
gourds, other forms: shapes of the fingers.
it was here. it was also here

what took place was very possible
without restive rankle of grass, water, sky, hills.

at nagoya

for Kyoko

there is a zoo & botanic gardens combined.
the vernal equinox comes on grey & subdued,
a curiously fluid morning, spring not fully arrived
& things go on their own ways. in the hothouses,
unforced, the theme is verdant crisis.

suave wind, tepid sun outside. bottled,
the heavy-lidded fuschias could explode,
extemporize the greenness of the year & bring with it
a pain, out in the open, need not be endured.

a high pile of glass with its own weather.
a thick pile of clothes with its own arms.
huge cactuses, boys' prickly heads potted.
the steely air lades moisture to the eyes.

where, at nagoya, a zoo & botanic gardens combine,
a portion of time lies waiting.

i can't remember where

i can't remember where, in some part of tokyo,
ripples of water were ringing outwards
in clear cool shivers. again the pond stilled.

a vagrant lying thickly wrapped on a bench;
splinters of sunlight, filtering through a paulownia,
soft-etched his stubbled face orange.

the cackle of wild ducks, fleeing or fled.
a nearby shrine, a tree's slender branches
tied all over with paper charms. a few people
in unhurry. a little rusty bell among grass
didn't tinkle, twice i shook it & threw it
into the pond; hardly a ripple. i peered into it,
my face somewhat startled. a nervous laugh,
as if not from me.

when memory is too much, one turns to the eye;
so i watch the particularities.
in a few days, i shall be going to osaka.
here, a deep contentment is, at once
i want to leave & never look back.
i know it all now; it was closer then.

a peony display, ueno park

how quaint, this woman standing elegantly
& this lush flower a foot below her face.
she turned, the flower bowed.
she sat on a stool, the flower sat
for her brush & reappeared
a soggy sea-anemone.
i suddenly laughed, regretted; the look
of her annoyance, the flower's arrogance.

the afternoon grown heavy,
amidst so many milling people
everything so still, hushed, revered.
yet the peonies maddened the ground
& providence had excluded all other flowers
for them to culminate in grace
& reappear in everybody's face.
they, peonies walked all about.
i sat & watched & watched;
it was time to go.

i walked into a fair at the first corner turned;
it was noise, silent spaces, both linked
by running children. a heavy peony-roiled sky
brimmed over with petals of rain.
everything was a quiet refrain
invisibly tethered to one will.

i am not sure

i am not sure; having walked a half hour
probably in a circle, i'm back here
near the coffee bar. the owner had once given me
a red tobacco cigarette. it was on a poster
&, not knowing japanese, had looked at it
long & hard & hearing some explanation
i couldn't understand, it was given me.
i had puffed it at toranomon station.

here is toranomon, & where shall i go?
the long lines of stalls at ueno? seafood,
pickles, fruit, vegetables. i think of the words
orenzi & ringo; not of the paradoxes of oranges
& apples. didn't think it clever. hachiko,
the statue of a dog, at shibuya station?

at the ginza; a side street, the aroma of corn-cobs
blew enticingly from an open wooden cart.
a florist's, bunches of baby's-breath like froth.
displays of food in glass cases; a replica salad
on which perched an iparella leaf.

tokyo is much much for me. i want to leave.
i want to leave without having left
& walk every side street & hear the slurps
the stand-up noodle shops emit.
at the hotel, i dreamt i was in tokyo
&, waking up, was, knew it was time to go
before the tentative become conditional.
& my sleep was without shadows.

a list of things

A MARKET AT UENO

gesticulating fingers of lentil, unwriggly eels,
spearheads of bamboo shoot, soothing water chestnuts,
green snakes of cucumber, jetsams of seaweed,
wrinkled-nose pickles, earspans of brown mushroom,
calm persimmons, outlandish roly-poly apples,
air-licking clams, dry earth-crusts of fish,
icy-eyed bream, powdered kabuki faces of cake,
paragraphs of beancurd, exhaling piles of garlic,
enpurpled piccolo noses of aubergine, lazy grapes,
no-nonsense tangerines, arms-folded-over squid,
shrine-pillars of celery, bullets of green chillie,
hibernating squares of handkerchief, fat tabi,
expandable sweaters, ventilated t-shirts, healthy cod,
alliterative clogs, knobbly topshell, discusses of sole,
lumpy puffy octopus, cheap skate, tight-jaw oysters,
brisk aprons, tough-guy pork, sectional ropes of radish,
whispery crinkled lettuce, placid sweet potatoes,
smarting capsicum, defiant crabs, sensuous musk melons,
humpy peanuts, leathery heels of abalone,
aerial spring onion, hour-glass pears, rotund avocados,
rib-caged pumpkins, chlorophyllic piles of iparella,
grumpy red mullet, macho beef, sassy tomatoes

are all there.

paired stills

at heian shrine
a handpainted kimono
rustled like wild grass

grass sprang from the hem
stopping short of the obi
& walked up those steps

gulls mewing loudly
carry the sunset
from here onto there

there, as seen from here,
banks of white chrysanthemums
spread a slow dawn

those single-peonies
within the reach of our fingers
tantalize the eye

those double-peonies
aching under their own weight
eye us wearily

the slope to the house
is paved with good intentions
to be kind to our feet

so walk up the slope
the house rises on its feet
welcomes us kindly

woman at the bench
two big parcels by her side
her two big achievements

two men at her side
her temporary parcels
their big achievement

so still, butterfly
you are regenerative
a perched amethyst

your eggs on the leaf
soon will spin cocoons & breeze
& so many loves

the riverside inn
serves many little dishes
remarkable us

a brown- green teacup
big as a rather small head
i hold it to mine

right in the centre
red roses named samurai
the rest were rōnin

even though it's may
a pink camellia
makes its own statement

raked patterns on sand
a little flaw at the swirls
gave it more merit

a white paper cup
thrown among michaelmas daisies
multiplied quickly

at this potter's house
we were offered fried bracken
gathered from the hills

i bought a bottle
picked bracken & mushroom
it contained my hill

the loud clamseller
praises the size of his clams
which grin openly

those baleful fisheyes
but much later it was i
who dreamt of the sea

waterbabies

And what did the little girl teach Tom? She taught him, first, what you have been taught ever since you said your first prayers at your mother's knees; but she taught him more simply. For the lessons in that world, my child, have no such hard words in them as the lessons in this, and therefore the waterbabies like them better than you like your lessons, and long to learn them more and more; and grown men cannot puzzle nor quarrel over their meaning, as they do here on land; for those lessons rise clear and pure...out of the everlasting ground of all life and truth.

Charles Kingsley, The Water Babies

other parts of the city, too, are capable of evoking the past
for anyone wishing to walk his imagination a little.
these klongs suggest the riverine quantity of life:
wooden huts opening on the water like brown teeth,
theatre sets of a different itinerant age.
buoyant clumps of water hyacinth, tenacious,
hard to separate limb from limb. spawns of water baby
-snails, flotsam, jetsam, cartons printed with bold figures
& colours, variously sinking annealing french letters.

the waterbabies, not to mince meat, are bouyant baby
   tenderloins.
each ensconced in a little boat with a canopy, curtains
& a smile, all drawn discreetly for any descending tom.
a tom descends a bridge. a boat is a vehicle for a tom.
a tenderloin is on the mat. a boy stands at the back,
wielding a long oar, the range of dark water. at the front,
an oil lamp bobs, lit for interaction. & to all this,
a little bridge is a major requirement.

one night, & we walk the night in the bridging
   imagination
of our mind. we imagine that interaction must have been

very inactive. five or six boats left their bridge,
left the bridging imagination of our mind, and drifted
aimlessly, lanterns bright. all at once, in the darkness,
a waterbaby started crying a plaintive song whose heart
-torn appeal was clear as a bell. another took up the song,
another, the others. in a moment, a full able-bodied
    choir,
a sweet clear siren that reached out nowhere &
    everywhere
& destroyed no one. they were not destroyed that one
    night.
slowly, the bell rippled into the inner vortex of the water.
somewhere, it is still alongside every pecky minor bridge.

denpasar

not surprisingly the bus was brand new.
at the lean-to junction, an assortment of visitors
boarded & then waited. i had expected more from kuta,
one said to her friend. excuse me, the interrupter
had expected less. what do you think denpasar will be like?
we were going there, our next evaluation.

a boy pedlar, hands & shoulders laden,
his face framing every low window.
cheap, can give discount. what's that? someone pointed
&, turning round, added: i don't go for all that
souvenir crap. what do you want it for? me, i go
for the real yield of the country.
a jam jar, that what's-that, round the boy's waist,
two grasshoppers caught in between waylaying buses.
not for sell.
but that's just what i want.
ok, how much? the boy was adept at extracting rupiahs,
lots & lots of which signified nearly nothing.

denpasar. out onto a square, a perfect square
of brown earth; grass was thoroughly absent.
ah, the grasshopper asked, perhaps seeing
in it whatever he wanted: & you know what?
we knew as, at once, he ripped off the string-tied leaf
& the grasshoppers sprang away after several feeble leaps.
what you do that for? not surprisingly:
to give them their freedom. what else you think?
i thought i saw people & insects hobble-hop, hobble-hop
over the burning earth. their freedom, it was true,
was right under the generosity of the hot hot sun
right over the world at bali.

cianjur

the woman & buffalo at a distance were so still.
rice seedlings would have grown from her fingers
if she had not hurried on. an extravagant sunset.
lush flowers, the decaying smell of the wooden house;
rotting balcony, moss-legged cane furniture.
the serial chirping of insects. a naked bulb,
later lit; the pool of ants' wings a prayer mat,
this day's announcement of approaching darkness
thick & crepy as a physicality.

the inside of the house was its outside in reverse.
clumsier rotting furniture. nothing worked, dry taps,
the telephone in a smoulder of dust.
an empty, empty hoariness; & its own despair.

all around the house, tall trees, vine-clung,
wild jasmine located by scent, chequer-board
padi fields. slope upon slope,
undulating till the last touched a level
& took away with its splendour one's breath;
a sere coconut leaf javelined the ground.
runner plants fingered their way &,
touching the house variously, never let go.

the distant orange sun taught different greens
for different identities. acid-green seedlings,
sunsteeped tree greens, brown greens, orange greens,
the violent green of a streaking kingfisher.
green noises from wet fields;
the eeriness floating off the hills, green ghosts.

& green were we when we got here
miles from anywhere, this dilapidation
described to us as a chalet-style hotel;
this ruin being hugged by all this grandeur
& gradually being strangled for not being a part.
matually encroaching, it could not vanquish.
it could be vanquished.
it could be very vanquished
before our eyes.

Notes

from *Only Lines*

one road — *page* 7
ch'ah, segamat, gemas, tampin - towns in Johore, Malaysia

panchor — 8
panchor - a town in Johore, Malaysia
rambutan - a tropical fruit
sultan - Muslim ruler

garden episode — 9
amah - domestic worker
samfoo - traditional attire for Chinese women

old house at ang siang hill — 16
ang siang hill - a district in Singapore

in passing — 17
k.l. - Kuala Lumpur, the capital of Malaysia

cameron highlands — 22
cameron highlands - a hill resort in Malaysia

balancing sounds — 23
brinchang, tanah rata - townships in Cameron Highlands

from *Commonplace*

everything's coming up numbers — 46
mah-piew-poh - a paper showcasing horse-racing and lottery results

an afternoon nap — 60
2nd lang. - second language
p.e. - physical exercise

group dynamics II — 70
pre-u - pre-university classes
bedok - a residential area in Singapore
bodoh - idiot

from *Down The Line*

medium	*page* 76
kampung - village	
traffic	96
park street - a street in Sydney	
at balmain	99
balmain - a district in Sydney	
i think (a book of changes)	100
straits times - an English newspaper in Singapore	
nanyang siang pau - a Chinese newspaper in Singapore	
2 mothers in an h d b playground	101
h d b - Housing Development Board, Singapore	
jamban - toilet	
toa-soh - sister-in-law	102
ah pah - father	
chya-hong - 'eat breeze' (literal); in this case, it means 'to have a leisurely drive'	
fiscal ear	103
kai lan - a leafy vegatable	

from *Man Snake Apple*

paraphrase	129
hākone - a city in Japan	
a good poem	130
mimiu - a restaurant in Japan	
udon suki - a dish prepared with noodles	
the shisen-do	131
sozu - a device made of bamboo; its clacking sound frightens off animals	
12-times table	132
gifu - a city in Japan	
i can't remember where	134
paulownia - a tree with a wide spread	

i am not sure *page* 136
toronomon - a district in Tokyo
orenzi - oranges
ringo - apples
hachiko - a dog famous for its loyalty; a bronze statue
was set up at Shibuya station to commemorate this

a list of things 137
kabuki - Japanese theatre
tabi - socks

paired stills 138
kimono - a long flowing Japanese gown
obi - sash for the kimono
samurai - member of the military cast in old Japan 139
rōnin - rogue samurai

waterbabies 140
klongs - canals in Bangkok

denpasar 142
kuta - a beach district in Bali
denpasar - the capital of Bali
cianjur 143
cianjur - a town in Indonesia

SKOOB *Pacifica*

Contemporary writings of the Pacific Rim and South Asia

Skoob Pacifica is a series which brings to a wider reading public the best in contemporary fiction, poetry, drama and criticism from the countries of the Pacific Rim. The flagship of the series, the *Skoob Pacifica Anthology*, presents selections from many of our featured authors alongside those of more established names.

SKOOB PACIFICA ANTHOLOGY No.1
S.E.Asia Writes Back!
Edited by I.K.Ong & C.Y.Loh

An eclectic blend of prose, poetry, drama and reportage which creates a vibrant picture of the post-colonial world. Featured writers include Vikram Seth, Yukio Mishima and Wole Soyinka, with short stories by Yasunari Kawabata and Derek Walcott.
ISBN 1 871438 19 5   Pbk   432pp   UK£5.99   US$10.95

SKOOB PACIFICA ANTHOLOGY No.2
The Pen Is Mightier Than The Sword

This second anthology focuses on exciting and challenging writing from Malaysia and Singapore in the 1990s. Also featured are pieces by Han Suyin, Toni Morrison and V.S. Naipaul.
ISBN 1 871438 54 3   Pbk   412pp   £6.99 $11.95

WRITING S.E./ASIA IN ENGLISH
Against The Grain
Shirley Geok-lin Lim

Shirley Geok-Lin Lim's penetrating essays demonstrate that local speech, national language and national canons have much to tell us about place and religion and the nations of the imagination.
ISBN 1 871438 49 7 Pbk   £224pp   12.99 $14.95

AVAILABLE FROM ALL GOOD BOOKSHOPS
OR ORDER FROM SKOOB BOOKS WITH A CREDIT CARD, TEL 020 7 404 3063 DELIVERY POST FREE IN U.K.
A DISCOUNT OF 20% IS AVAILABLE WHEN YOU ORDER TWO BOOKS OR MORE, DIRECT FROM SKOOB.

THE RETURN
K.S. Maniam

Set against the dramatic backdrop of Malaysian independence, this novel of magical realism has become a modern classic.
ISBN 1 871438 04 7   Pbk 208pp   UK£5.99   US$10.95

IN A FAR COUNTRY
K.S. Maniam

This compelling novel, a potent cocktail of cultures, race and religion, examines the dilemmas at the heart of multicultural life.
ISBN 1 871438 14 4   Pbk 224pp   £5.99 $10.95

SENSUOUS HORIZONS
Four stories and four plays
K.S. Maniam

Eight works which are thematically linked and represent a new departure for the author as he explores the darker side of the Malaysian psyche.
ISBN 1 871438 69 1   Pbk 262pp   £6.99 $11.95

HAUNTING THE TIGER
K.S. Maniam

A collection of thirteen stories which spans the career of a myth maker over the last twenty years.
ISBN 1 871438 79 9   Pbk 232pp   £6.99

IN THE NAME OF LOVE
Ramli Ibrahim

First performed in 1991, *In the Name of Love* has enjoyed critical and popular success. It is comprised of three monologues for a single actress, touching upon such themes as coming to terms with loss and confrontations with the past.
ISBN 1 871438 24 1   Pbk 104pp   £6.99 $11.95

AVAILABLE FROM ALL GOOD BOOKSHOPS
OR ORDER FROM SKOOB BOOKS WITH A CREDIT CARD, TEL 020 7 404 3063 DELIVERY POST FREE IN U.K.
A DISCOUNT OF 20% IS AVAILABLE WHEN YOU ORDER TWO BOOKS OR MORE, DIRECT FROM SKOOB.

poetry from
SKOOB BOOKS LTD

MONSOON HISTORY
Selected Poems
Shirley Geok-lin Lim

Intelligent writing that offers insight, humour and a sense of far away places. The first UK collection from an international prize winning poet. Her belief in the acceptance of cultural multiplicity is reflected in work that reflects her Malaysian childhood and family but also casts a coolly observant eye over America, where she now lives and works.

ISBN 1 871438 44 6 Pbk 200pp UK£6.99 US$11.95

WAYS OF EXILE
Poems from the First Decade
Wong Phui Nam

This collection traces the development of the poet, honouring the Malaysian soul as well as the geographical and spiritual ground of his country. These verses subtly interweave feelings of fear, ennui, optimism and nostalgia.

ISBN 1 871438 09 8 Pbk 176pp £5.99 $11.95

WHERE WE ARE
Selected Poems and Zen Translations
Lucien Stryk

Stryk's poetry, bounded by Zen, embodies a way of inhabiting a specific moment. This new collection contains a balanced selection from poetry written over a period of forty years. Some are long out of print, others receiving their first publication. It includes award winning translations of Japanese and Chinese Zen masters.

ISBN 1 871438 03 9 Pbk 178pp £8.95 $12.95

AVAILABLE FROM ALL GOOD BOOKSHOPS
OR ORDER FROM SKOOB BOOKS WITH A CREDIT CARD, TEL 020 7 404 3063 DELIVERY POST FREE IN U.K.
A DISCOUNT OF 20% IS AVAILABLE WHEN YOU ORDER TWO BOOKS OR MORE, DIRECT FROM SKOOB.

COLLECTED JOURNALS 1936 - 42
David Gascoyne

These journals illuminate and complement Gascoyne's poetry and reaffirm him as a major poetic voice of the twentieth century. "In many of the entries there are to be found the seeds of the great metaphysical poems that he was to compose later... Skoob Books...are to be congratulated." *The Tablet*

ISBN 1 871438 50 0 Pbk 402pp UK£10.99 US$19.95

AUTOBIOGRAPHIES
Kathleen Raine

Opening with a magical evocation of childhood in a remote Northumbrian hamlet during the First World War, *Autobiographies* is an illuminating attempt to chart the inner life of one of the most eminent poets of our time.

ISBN 1 871438 41 1 Pbk 348pp £12.99 $24.95

STRING OF BEGINNINGS
Intermittent Memoirs 1924 - 1954
Michael Hamburger

A witty and thoughtful autobiography, this is the frank and entertaining story of one of the most powerful poets and translators working today.

"Fine and memorable" *Poetry Review*

ISBN 1 871438 66 7 Pbk 338pp £10.99 $19.95

PIGEONS AND MOLES
Selected Writings
Gunter Eich
Translated by Michael Hamburger

Introducing a sceptical, witty and anarchic poet to British readers, with the first substantial selection from Eich's bitter and graceful poems, his acclaimed radio plays and the controversial late prose poems.

ISBN 1 871438 81 0 Pbk 208pp £7.99 (Not in USA)

AVAILABLE FROM ALL GOOD BOOKSHOPS
OR ORDER FROM SKOOB BOOKS WITH A CREDIT CARD, TEL 020 7404 3063 DELIVERY POST FREE IN U.K.
A DISCOUNT OF 20% IS AVAILABLE WHEN YOU ORDER TWO BOOKS OR MORE, DIRECT FROM SKOOB.

COLLECTED POEMS
George Eliot

Edited with an Introduction by Lucien Jenkins

George Eliot's poetry has been unjustly neglected for over a century. Whether she is writing evocatively of rural childhood, as in the sonnets, or passionately engaged with the issues of nationalism and racial prejudice in her ambitious epic *The Spanish Gypsy*, Eliot is a wonderful and surprising poet.

Hbk ISBN 1 871438 35 7 490pp UK£18.95 US$35

THE SONNETS TO ORPHEUS
Rainer Maria Rilke

Translated by Leslie Norris and Alan Keele

Rilke's sonnet sequence, here in a fresh translation, ranks amongst the greatest works of modern literature, exploring the meaning of death and the value of art.

ISBN 1 871438 60 8 Pbk 80pp £5.99 (Not in USA)

PERSONAE
and other selected poems

Peter Abbs

This is a collection of ironic, poignant and epigrammatic poems informed by imaginative experience, whether of mythical characters, poets, philosophers or artists. the volume is balanced by a selection of work from a period of fifteen years including the much praised *Icons of Time*.

ISBN 1 871438 77 2 Pbk 176pp £8.99 $19.95

THE POLEMICS OF IMAGINATION
Selected Essays on Art, Culture and Society

Peter Abbs

These essays offer a personal critique of education, culture and society in modern Britain. Employing his own experiences as well as illuminating analysis of Eliot, Pound, Edmund Gosse and others, he has produced a remarkable collection.

ISBN 1871438 31 4 Pbk 174pp £8.95 $14.95

AVAILABLE FROM ALL GOOD BOOKSHOPS
OR ORDER FROM SKOOB BOOKS WITH A CREDIT CARD, TEL 020 7 404 3063 DELIVERY POST FREE IN U.K.
A DISCOUNT OF 20% IS AVAILABLE WHEN YOU ORDER TWO BOOKS OR MORE, DIRECT FROM SKOOB.